TRAGEDIES OI BLANCO

A Story of the Texas Panhandle

By

Captain Robert Goldthwaite Carter

U.S. ARMY

QUAN-AH PARKER
PRINCIPAL WAR CHIEF OF THE QUA-HA-DA COMANCHES

Tragedies of Cañon Blanco

The Texas Panhandle

It is nearly fifty years since these tragedies occurred. There are few survivors. The writer is, perhaps, the only one. This is written in the vague hope that this chronicle of the events of that period may possibly prove of some lasting and, perhaps, historical value to posterity.

The country all about the scene of these tragical events—the Texas Panhandle—was then wild, unsettled, covered with sage brush, scrub oak and chaparral, and its only inhabitants were Indians, buffalo, lobo wolves, coyotes, jack-rabbits, prairie-dogs and rattlesnakes, with here and there a few scattered herds of antelope. The railroad, that great civilizing agency, the telegraph, the telephone, and the many other marvelous inventions of man, have wrought such a wonderful transformation in our great western country that the American Indian will, if he has not already, become a race of the past, and history alone will record the remarkable deeds and strange career of an almost extinct people. With these miraculous changes has come the total extermination of the buffalo—the Indians' migratory companion and source of living—and pretty much all of the wild game that in almost countless numbers freely roamed those vast prairies. Where now the railroads girdle that country the nomadic redman lived his free and careless life and the bison thrived and roamed undisturbed at that period—where are now the appliances of modern civilization, and prosperous communities, then nothing but desolation reigned for many miles around. In the expansion and peopling of this vast country, our little Army was most closely identified. In fact, it was the pioneer of civilization. The life was full of danger, hardships, privations, and sacrifices, little known or appreciated by the present generation. Our only water was obtained from the buffalo wallow-holes—stagnant, warm, and nauseating, odorous with smells, and covered with a green slime which had to be pushed aside—or from the Brazos River, the Double Mountain Fork of the Brazos, and their many small tributaries, all strongly impregnated with gypsum, which was but a trifle better. The Indians carried all of the water they used, in crossing the Staked Plains, in buffalo paunches packed upon the mules.

Where populous towns, ranches and well-tilled farms, grain fields, orchards, and oil "gushers" are now located, with railroads either running through or near them, we were making trails, upon which the main roads now run, in search of hostile savages, for the purpose of punishing them or compelling them to go into the Indian reservations, and to permit the settlers, then held back by the murderous acts of these redskins, to advance and spread the civilization of the white man throughout the western tiers of counties in that far-off western panhandle of Texas.

The Old Mackenzie Trail

Stretching onward toward the sunset.
    O'er prairie, hill, and vale,
Far beyond the Double Mountains
    Winds the old Mackenzie Trail.

Ah, what thoughts and border memories
    Does that dreaming trail suggest;
Thoughts of travelers gone forever
    To the twilight realms of rest.

Where are now the scouts and soldiers,
    And those wagon-trains of care,
Those grim men and haggard women?
    And the echoes whisper—Where?

Ah, what tales of joys and sorrows
    Could that silent trail relate:
Tales of loss, and wrecked ambitions.
    Tales of hope, of love, and hate;

Tales of hunger, thirst, and anguish.
    Tales of skulking Indian braves.
Tales of fear, and death, and danger.

Tales of lonely prairie graves.

Where are now that trail's processions
    Winding westward sure and slow?
Lost! Ah, yes; destroyed by progress,
    Gone to realms of long ago.

Nevermore shall bold Mackenzie,
    With his brave and dauntless band.
Guide the restless, roving settlers
    Through the Texas borderland.

Yes! that soldiers' work is over,
    And the dim trail rests at last;
But his name and trail still lead us
    Through the borders of the past.

This is cited to show how the efforts of our gallant and hard-toiling little Regular Army of that period in aid of that far-off, wild, unsettled country—then absolutely closed tight to the white man—has borne fruit. But, alas! how little credit for standing as a bulwark for such a civilization and achieving such astonishing changes has been given to the men who accomplished it.

Cañon Blanco

Cañon Blanco in northwestern Texas, the so-called Texas Panhandle, extends through parts of three counties—Crosby, Floyd, and Hale. Through it flows a small quicksand stream called Catfish Creek, and sometimes the cañon itself has been called Catfish Cañon. Mount Blanco, or more properly the butte at the mouth of the cañon, where the creek joins the Freshwater Fork of the Brazos, was where these tragedies occurred.

Near here are the small towns of Blanco, Palo Duro, Floydada to the north, McAdoo a few miles east, and to the northwest, on the A. T. & S. F. system, are Canyon and Happy, while almost due north and about twelve miles from the Tule "Canyon," which was an old Indian hiding place, is the considerable town or city of Amarillo in Potter County, at the junction of the C. R. I. & G., P. & S. F., and A. T. & S. F. systems. This town has not only been a rich and productive wheat center, millions of dollars' worth having been marketed annually, but it and the surrounding country to the south and southeast has become one of the greatest oil centers of the United States, if not of the world, the Ranger and Burkburnett fields during recent oil booms having made many millionaires, besides wrecking many would-be speculators.

In Cañon Blanco, Tule "Canyon," Quit-a-Que (*Keet-a-Kay*), and about the headwaters of the Pease River, there had dwelt for many years a nomadic band of savages, known as the Qua-ha-da Comanches (taken from Comanche-Kwaina, signifying "vagrant"). They were the implacable enemies of the whites, and this hatred had been handed down for many years.

The Comanches

The Comanches are divided into several bands the same as the Sioux, each band owing allegiance to and bearing social, economic and political relations to the tribe proper. There were the Cost-che-teght-kas (or buffalo eaters), the Pen-e-teght-kas (or honey eaters), the No-konees (or wanderers), the Yam-per-i-cos (or root diggers), and last came the Qua-ha-das of the Staked Plains ("Llano Estacado"), the Chatz-ken-ners (or antelope users). The three first bands, broken up, are Moo-chas (or "Crooked Mountain" band), the Ten-na-was (or "Liver-eaters") and Tea-chatz-ken-nas (or "Servers"). The middle Comanches were the Yam-per-i-cos, and the southern Comanches were the Comanches proper.

This story deals entirely with the Qua-ha-da band, the famous Chatz-ken-nas, or antelope-users, of the Staked Plains. This band had, for many years, been isolated from the tribe, having refused to enter into the "Medicine Lodge" Treaty of 1867, by which the Comanches, Ki-o-was, Apaches, Cheyennes, and Arapahos were assigned to reservations, and until 1875, four years after this tragedy, were roaming outside of any designated reservation or abiding place. They were free-lances in a partially civilized region. Everything was open to their bloody and frequent incursions.

In 1836 the principal war chief of the Qua-ha-das was Peta Nacona (the "Wanderer"). It was then the wildest and most hostile band of the Comanche tribe, and the most inveterate raiders on the Texas border.

Parker's Fort—The Romance of Quanah

On May 19, 1836, a few days after the battle of San Jacinto was fought, these Indians, under Nacona, raided Parkers Fort, situated at the headwaters of Navasota Creek—a tributary of the Brazos—near where the town of that name is now located, sixty miles from the nearest white settlement, and two miles from the present town of Groesbeck, Limestone County, Texas. The post was occupied by six men and several women and children. The Indians shrewdly presented a white flag, and sent some of their number to the post to say they were friendly.

One of the inmates, Benjamin Parker (who was the father of Cynthia Ann Parker and the grandfather of Chief Quanah Parker), let them enter the fort, believing that they were friendly Indians and wanted to make a treaty with the whites, but when he was within their power they treacherously attacked and killed him and immediately captured the fort.

It was a stockade fort, occupied by several families who had just returned from the flight before the Mexican army, commanded by General Santa Ana. After effecting an entrance into Parkers Fort by pretending to be friendly, the Indians massacred all the men and some of the women and children, carrying away captive Mrs. Plummer and her son, two years old; Mrs. Kellogg; Cynthia Ann Parker, then nine years old, and her brother, aged six. After leaving the fort the Comanches and Kiowas traveled together until midnight. They then camped, brought their prisoners together, tied their hands behind them so tightly as to cut the flesh, tied their feet together, and threw them on their faces; then gathered around with the bloody scalps they had taken at the fort and commenced their war dance. They danced, screamed, yelled, and stamped upon the prisoners, beating them with bows until the blood flowed from their bruises, and the rest of the night the women had to listen to the cries and groans of the little children. When the tribes parted each of the bands took a captive.

Cynthia Ann Parker was claimed by the Comanche tribe, and became their permanent captive. Nothing was heard from her for many years, but in the meantime her relatives and friends and the Texas authorities did everything in their power to ascertain her fate and secure her release, if she was living.

In the autumn of 1860 the Comanches, in force under their chief, Peta Nacona, the father of Quanah Parker and the Indian husband of Cynthia Ann, raided through Parker and adjoining counties and inflicted great distress upon the white settlements.

But in December he was followed and surprised in his own camp on Pease River by a force of forty Texas Rangers and twenty dragoons of the Regular Army, in all sixty soldiers, under Captain "Sul" Ross, of the Rangers. His camp was captured and many slain. The chief fled at full speed, with another Indian behind him on the same horse, and his wife, with an infant in her arms, on a fleet pony beside him. The captain of the Rangers, with one attendant, pursued. They soon overtook the chief's wife, who held up her child and stopped. Leaving her with his attendant, the captain pursued the two Indians on one horse, and, coming up with them, fired with his heavy revolving pistol, killing the hindmost. The same ball would have also killed the chief, but his shield hanging on his back prevented. The hindmost, in falling, dragged the chief from his horse, but he lit upon his feet and plied his pursuers with arrows, wounding his horse. The wound set the animal to rearing and plunging so violently that the ranger could not aim his weapon. Victory in the single combat seemed on the point of declaring for the savage. His well-directed arrows were sent rapidly; but a random shot from the Ranger broke his right arm and disabled him, both hands being indispensable to the use of the bow.

The captain's horse becoming quiet, he shot the chief twice through the body, who then walked deliberately to a tree near by and, leaning against it, began to sing a wild, weird song—the death song of his tribe, a custom in many tribes in the presence of certain death. The captain's men coming up with an interpreter, the chief was summoned to surrender, but he answered by a savage thrust at the captain with his lance held in his left hand. It was plain that he would surrender only to death. The captain directed one of his attendants to "finish him," and the death song ended. The Indian who had been riding behind the chief proved to be a young female, but her sex was not distinguished in the flight, because she was covered with a buffalo robe with only the head visible. The woman taken with the child, the fallen chief's wife, was seen to be a white woman, and she had blue eyes. She wept incessantly and the captain directed the interpreter to tell her that they recognized her as one of their own nation and would not hurt her. She replied that she was not weeping for herself, but for her two boys, who were in the battle, and, she feared, were slain. She was sent to the white settlement, where she was speedily identified as Cynthia Ann Parker, who was captured when nine years old by the Comanches at Parkers Fort massacre in 1836. She was not reconciled to civilization, and had to be watched to prevent her escape. Her little child, named Prairie Flower, died, and in less than two years she died also and was laid beside her little barbarian. Of her sons, one died on the plains, but the other lived and became the famous chief, Quanah Parker.

This battle ground was but about twenty miles above the town of Vernon, on Pease River, at the mouth of Mule Creek and in Foard County, Texas.

There have been many wild newspaper stories and legends concerning the capture of Cynthia Ann Parker. One was that she was taken in 1790 on the banks of the Scioto River, near the present site of Chillicothe, Ohio, and that her parents were from Virginia, etc.

The story, as the writer relates it, is not only official but absolutely reliable, coming as it does from the gallant Ranger, Captain Ross, who afterwards became a brigadier-general in the Confederate Army, and subsequently governor of the State of Texas. He died some fifteen or eighteen years ago, universally beloved by all Texans. While serving as governor he gave to Hon. John H. Stephens, M. C, all the particulars regarding her capture.

Quanah himself knew but little about the early life of his mother, or when and where she was captured.

Quanah was born about 1845. He grew up with the Qua-ha-da band, and on the death of his father, Nacona, rapidly rose to more or less commanding influence as principal war chief of that band, as well as in the Comanche tribe.

In 1871 the band was still out under Quanah, moving about from place to place, but generally near the headwaters of Pease River, their old stamping ground, the Palo Duro Cañon, in Cañon Blanco, and near the mouth of McClellan's Creek, a small tributary of the north fork of the Red River, although he was associated in these raids, reports of which were constantly reaching us, with Mow-wi (the "Handshaker") and Para-a-coom ("He Bear"); both subchiefs of the Qua-ha-da band. The village of Mow-wi, on McClellan's Creek, was destroyed in September, 1872, by our command operating from Fort Richardson, Texas.

The Fourth Cavalry had been out in the field from May 1 until about September 13, 1870, much of the time north of Red River in the Indian Territory (now Oklahoma), by direction of General Sherman, and had succeeded in driving in the Kiowas under Ton-ne-un-co ("Kicking Bird"), who had fled from the Fort Sill reservation in May of that year when he (General Sherman) had ordered the arrest at Fort Sill of the principal chiefs of that tribe, including the notorious war chiefs, See-ti-toh (Sa-tan-ta, "White Bear") and Quirl-par-ko ("Lone Wolf"), for the massacre of seven teamsters a few weeks before on Salt Creek prairie, two miles from Rock Creek Station, near Fort Richardson, Texas. Had a strong guard not been stationed in General Grierson's quarters, concealed from view, when General Sherman ordered their arrest at a council which was being held, he would have been killed through the treachery of the Indians, who went to the conference with arms concealed under their blankets, but were foiled by General Sherman's precautions. It came very near, however, to being another General Canby murder. The writer has a copy of General Sherman's letter written at that period, graphically describing the scene.

After having accomplished this duty of stampeding Kicking Bird into Fort Sill, in which we were ably (?) assisted by General Grierson, who, either through jealousy or fear, sent his post interpreter, Horace P. Jones, into Kicking Bird's camp on the Sweetwater—near where old Fort Elliott was later located—to warn him that the "Great Chief from Texas, Mackenzie, was about to attack him outside of the reservation, and to get in as soon as possible," and hearing that the Comanches had been raiding down the country again, and had already secured many horses, cattle, and, as rumor had it, killed some people and captured women and children, among them a child five years of age, Mackenzie determined to pay his attention now to the Indians of the Texas Panhandle in their fastnesses, the breaks and small cañons of the Staked Plains.

Camp Cooper—The Rendezvous

On September 19, therefore, we left Fort Richardson again for a new campaign. We concentrated and reorganized at old Camp Cooper on Tecumseh's Creek, a small tributary of the Clear Fork of the Brazos, about five miles from Fort Griffin, Texas. General Robert E. Lee built this post some years before the Civil War, and occupied it for some time. General John B. Hood, a general in the Confederate Army, saw his first service here. It was a former reservation for the southern Comanches, and, at this period, was in ruins. On August 12, Lawrie Tatum, the Quaker Indian agent at Fort Sill, wrote General Grierson as follows: "I should be very glad indeed if thee and General Mackenzie could get that little captive, and induce Mow-way (Mow-wi) and his band to come into the reservation and behave * * * Mow-way does not appear likely to bring in that poor little captive child of his own volition * * * I did not get a definite idea of where Mow-way is." * * * A copy of this letter was furnished to General Mackenzie, who then determined to definitely locate the Qua-ha-das, punish them, and, if possible, bring in the child.

On September 25, eight (8) companies (or troops) of the Fourth Cavalry (A, B, D, F, G, H, K, and L), and two (2) companies of the Eleventh Infantry (F and I), with about twenty Ton-ka-way scouts, were in camp near Fort Griffin. On that, night a big band of Indians came in to Murphy's ranch, about twenty miles from the post, and, it was reported, ran off a herd of one hundred and twenty cattle and thirteen horses, and two citizens, Stockton and James, part owners of this stock, joined us at our camp, ready to take up the trail of their animals, assist in punishing these depredators and murdering thieves, and to identify, if possibly, their brands, if secured. General Mackenzie had not then arrived, and the settlers showed signs of anger at Capt. Wirt Davis, commanding camp, because he would not order out the command at once and take up the trail. But he had positive orders from Mackenzie to remain at this camp resting the men and animals. Up to this period the writer had been field adjutant and a general *"Pooh Bah"* of the command—topographical engineer, etc.—but was now attached, first to "K" Troop (his own troop "E" having been left at Fort Richardson) and later to "B" Troop for duty, and to command it, as Captain Clarence Mauck of that troop now commanded the squadron, then composed of two troops.

On the morning of September 30 the writer was ordered to take eight men and five "Tonk" trailers or scouts, proceed up the Clear Fork, and select a good camp for the command and some kind of a practicable road for the wagon train. Upon his return, on October 3, we moved out. The writer rode at the head of the column, directing the scouts in advance, and guiding it over the trail he had made to the bend of the stream.

The March for the "Panhandle"—The "Double Mountain" Fork—A "Close Shave"

We left our bivouac on the beautiful bend of the Clear Fork the next morning, with about six hundred men and nearly one hundred pack mules, all in fine condition, although the horses were somewhat thin and worn by their long campaign since May. The Indian scouts, our faithful "Tonks," under Lieutenant P. M. Boehm, were far in advance, well fanned out, combing the country for trails, with a selected advance guard in close support if necessary, and to guard against surprise. All were cheerful, and our old song rang out, "Come home, John, don't stay long; Come home soon to your own Chick-a-biddy!" California and Paint Creeks, both quicksand streams, with rather steep banks and no regular fords, were crossed. Plenty of buffalo and antelope were seen on the flanks, but no hunting was now permitted. Other and different game was our objective. Mackenzie sent the writer to the rear several times to assist Lawton, our newly joined Regimental Quartermaster, in crossing these creeks and numerous "sloughs" or "arroyos," saying: "You men of the Civil War have had more experience in that work, in "speeding up" wagon trains, than my other and younger officers, and if you and Lawton can't make time I don't know who can."

Our next camp was but a few miles from the Double Mountains, which were in plain sight. Marching early the next morning we crossed the Double Mountain Fork of the Brazos, and at night camped near "Flat Top," or "Cottonwood Springs." Here we found the vilest water, but excellent grazing for the animals. We saw immense herds of buffalo all day, and at night we were literally in their midst, for they only moved off a mile or two for our accommodation, and to avoid the scent of our command coming down the wind. Only enough were killed to furnish fresh meat for the entire command, as was our custom. The writer was in charge of the guard that night. This included herd guards, "sleeping parties," all camp guards and picket outposts. Preparatory to midnight inspection of all the posts, he lay down in a buffalo robe near the sergeant in charge of the picket reserve, to protect himself from a cold wind that had now increased to a stiff gale, making it difficult to hear any sounds outside the camp. Suddenly, however, he heard above the din of the gale a tremendous tramping and an unmistakable snorting and bellowing. Placing his ear to the ground, he could hear it plainer, and this time there was a heavy jarring. Throwing off his robe, he could distinctly see coming through the darkness an immense, black, moving mass, which he knew at once were the herds of buffalo. They were making directly for the reserve and our horse herds which had inadvertently been staked or lariated directly across the paths or water trails leading to their usual drinking holes. There was no time to lose, even to alarm the sleeping camp. The writer did not dare to fire upon them to break the heads of the herds, as that might alarm and also stampede the horses, and besides orders had been given that no shots should be fired now that we were in the enemy's country. He jumped to his feet, shouted to the sergeant to rout out his guard, and to carry their blankets forward and, by meeting the mass, waving them, and yelling, to try and turn them aside. The men acted promptly and effectively. The immense herds of brown monsters were caromed off and they stampeded to our left at breakneck speed, rushing and jostling, but flushing only the edge of one of our horse herds, and were soon crowding down the banks to the flats below, thundering off in the black gloom of night with a noise that aroused every sleeper in camp, who supposed for a moment that our horses had broken away from their lariats and had gone. As we watched their grotesque shadows and brown masses troop off in the darkness in countless hundreds, with a noise like the mighty rumbling of thunder, making the ground fairly tremble with their tramping, one could hardly repress a shudder at what might have been the result of this nocturnal visit, for although the horses were strongly "lariated out," "staked" or "picketed," nothing could have saved them from the terror which this headlong charge would have inevitably created, had we not heard them just in time to turn the leading herds. It was a close shave, and might have proved a sad disaster.

The writer slept no more that night, but rolling himself in his buffalo robe tried to ward off the piercing wind.

Duck Creek—The Unsuccessful Scout

Moving early we reached Duck Creek—no water on the road, and our trail was mostly over a rolling prairie thinly covered with mesquite, but thickly covered with dog towns, populated by prairie-dogs, and immense herds of buffalo as far as the eye could reach. The water in the creek was clear, contained in large waterholes, all impregnated with gypsum, an improvement, however, over the last camp. We discovered this day the trading stations of the Mexicans with the Indians, consisting of curiously built caves in the high banks or bluffs, the earth being propped up or kept in place by a framework of poles, giving these subterranean abodes the appearance of grated prison doors or windows, reminding us of the cave dwellers of Arizona and New Mexico. These trading stations were now abandoned. At night, after much persuasion, the "Tonks" were sent out to find, if possible, any signs of the Comanche villages, it being Mackenzie's intention, as soon as they, the "Tonks" returned, to make a night march and surprise the enemy. Our Indian scouts were very timid when sent out in a new country without an escort or supporting column, for fear our own men might mistake them for hostiles, before they could be recognized, especially at night, and fire upon them.

Here we located our supply camp from which we could load the pack mules for mobility and quick movements in any direction; the two infantry companies to be left as a sufficient guard, and Lawton to control the supplies. Here the writer was directed to take a small detachment and scout to the head of the creek to reconnoiter for signs and, if possible, strike the trail of our "Tonks." It proved unsuccessful as our route was too far to the east.

Night March in the—"Bad Lands" for a Surprise—The Barrier

Upon our return the same day, Mackenzie announced his intention to strike out that night and make a quick march to surprise the hostiles. The wagons were therefore corraled or parked, the mules packed, and, without waiting for the return of the "Tonks," and under cover of darkness, leaving our cook fires to deceive the enemy, we started.

After many trials, tribulations, and much hard talk verging upon profanity, and many bruises, we all brought up at midnight in a small box cañon or break, against the high and rocky face of an impassible wall, which, in the inky blackness of a starless and moonless night, we could not see our way clear to scale, and unable to find any way out, after many rather comical scenes, floundering among the ravines and arroyas forming this barrier, we bivouacked without fires until morning, the heels of the pack mules sharply defining our limits, and the companies hardly moving from column as they halted, for fear of inextricable confusion and injury by accident. Cold "snacks" were all we could obtain for "eats." At daybreak, or just before it was fairly light, we moved by a flank around the obstacle, which we found too steep to climb, and after a rapid and hard march over rough country of about five hours we reached the Freshwater Fork of the Brazos River, the objective we ought to have gained at daylight. To our surprise the water was really fresh, and its name was not misleading. We unsaddled, built fires, and ate breakfast. Until now no signs of the missing Ton-ka-ways had been discovered; nothing was known thus far but what our march had been a success. Lieutenant Boehm recognized the spot as being near where Captain Carrol of the Ninth Cavalry and he had had a fight with this same band of Comanches the year before. A hasty reconnoissance revealed the brush huts or "wickey-ups," and remnants of lodges or "tepees" could be seen on high ground near the stream and to our left. In the early afternoon a squadron under Captain E. M. Heyl was sent out on a reconnoissance, while the balance of the command rested after their hard struggle of the previous night.

The "Tonks" Discover the Comanches

The "Tonk" scouts soon espied our column and came in, but while hastening along some ravines, on high ground, ran rather unexpectedly upon four Comanches, also busily intent upon watching our reconnoitering squadron, and our "surprise" (?) column. The "Tonks" gave chase, which, for a time, proved quite exciting, but the hostiles being better mounted soon distanced their pursuers and vanished into the hills. The scouts all looked the worse for wear, being fagged out, dirty, and with scalp-locks looking touzled and tangled. Having been without sleep or food since leaving our camp on Duck Creek, they were nearly famished and as ravenous as wolves.

They reported their belief in having discovered the trail leading to the Qua-ha-da village. At three p. m. the writer was detailed as officer-of-the-day, and immediately after the short ceremony of guard mount, word was passed along—"boots and saddle" never being sounded in an Indian country—for the command to "pack up." The column was soon in motion, and with a strong guard I followed in rear with the entire pack train of nearly one hundred mules. The Fresh Fork was full of quick-sands, and in crossing the train a number of the animals "bogged," which, fortunately, we got out upon dry land very soon, but not without hard work, and were just congratulating ourselves when a shot was heard, and then another, either at the head of the column, or of the pack train, now strung out at some length.

The main column was alarmed. Mackenzie came galloping to the rear, and with some excitement inquired where the shots came from, fearing that Captain Mauck's squadron, which had been sent back to the camp we had left, as a "blind," had been attacked. Without waiting to learn the cause of the shots, he directed the writer to ride at a gallop to the head of the column and tell Captain Wirt Davis to countermarch the command, and move it rapidly to the rear. Mackenzie, upon meeting it, however, after having ascertained that a careless soldier of the rear guard had discharged his piece, caused it to move to the front again. Much valuable time had been thus lost. The country was rough, with some foothills and small arroyas. Frequent halts were made and it was nearly dark before the command was straightened out and ready to go into camp.

The absent squadron was sent for, and under the shadow of some abrupt hills, scarcely one hundred yards from the stream, we went into bivouac. It was a pocket valley. The horses were "staked out" with "cross side lines," picket pins securely driven, and the men allowed to make small fires, which, in the writer's judgment, was a grave error, as will be seen. The missing squadron came in after dark, and, not finding much room, crowded pretty close to the rear company, the horses being somewhat huddled upon their grazing ground—another unfortunate error.

We were in a narrow pocket, with a line of small bluffs or foothills close to us on one side, and a treacherous quicksand stream on the other, with a wily enemy always to be accounted for—an excellent camp in time of peace, or even an ideal theoretical camp in time of war—*provided no Indians were about.*

The Midnight Alarm and Attack—Hell Breaks Loose!"

The pickets were posted, the necessary instructions were given, and, without taking my pistol off, loosening my belt, or removing my boots, but uncoiling my lariat and driving my picket pin close to my hand so that I could quickly seize it, my horse remaining saddled (the only one in the command), I lay down until time to inspect the posts. Nearby were Lieutenants P. M. Boehm and W. A. Thompson, and the two cattlemen, Stockton and James, already referred to, who were accompanying us to recover their stock.

It had been a most eventful day. Our thoughts were of the exciting incidents of the march at early dawn; reaching the Fresh Fork; the chase of the four Comanches by our scouts; the shot and rapid countermarch—but especially the poor camp we were now in. It was, in fact, a rapid review of this day's events, and we all made our comments.

It drew near midnight. All was still except the night noises of the horse herds grazing at the end of their lariats. Small fires had been allowed (another error of indulgence to the men), and a few slumbering embers of the one nearest to us flashed up, sparkled and died down, and all was dark, almost inky blackness, when suddenly a yell, followed by a shot, rang down the valley; then a succession of unearthly, bloodcuddling yells, a dozen shots in quick succession, one after the other, a rush, and, in an instant, our whole camp was aroused.

The camp was attacked! The rapid flashes of the carbines and pistols from the rear squadron, now in action, showed us, at intervals, that the ridge, or line of small foothills which skirted our entire camp, was alive with wild Indians, riding by at full speed, shaking dried buffalo robes, ringing bells, yelling like wild demons, and by every other possible device trying to stampede our animals. The answering whoops of our Ton-ka-ways and the loud bangs of carbines, with the shouts of the men, could now be heard, mingled with the hoarse commands of the officers, "Get to your horses!" For a few moments all was uproar and confusion, but above all this din of arms, yells, whoops of Indians and shouts of soldiers came another sound, like the rumbling of heavy thunder, never to be mistaken when once heard by a cavalry command, which told us all too surely but sadly that all of our horses were stampeding. Upon them was staked almost our very existence in this far-off wilderness. Unless checked, their total loss seemed inevitable. Now came the loud commands: "Every man to his lariat!" "Stand by your horses!"—heard amidst all the tumult.

The scene beggars all description by tongue or pen.

There was no "artist on the spot!" At every flash the horses and mules, nearly six hundred in number, could be seen rearing, jumping, plunging, running and snorting, with a strength that terror and brute frenzy alone can inspire. They trembled and groaned in their crazed fright, until they went down on their knees, straining all the time to free themselves from their lariats. As they plunged and became inextricably intermingled and more and more tangled up, the lariats could be heard snapping and crackling like the reports of pistols. Iron picket pins were hurtling, swishing, and whistling more dangerous than bullets. Men, crouching as they ran, vainly endeavored to seize the pins as they whirled and tore through the air, only to be dragged and thrown among the heels of the horses with hands lacerated and burnt by the ropes running rapidly through their fingers. To one who has never seen or heard a night stampede of horses, mules, or of buffalo such a description would give no adequate conception of this midnight debacle.

The herds thundered off in the distance; the men secured all they could.

The hissing and spitting of the bullets sounded viciously and the yells of the retreating Indians from the distance came back on the midnight air with a peculiar, taunting ring, telling all too plainly that the Qua-ha-das, Quanah's wild band of Comanches, had been among us.

We had found them at last! Or, at least, *they had found us!* The tangled masses of horses, lariats, picket pins, and side lines were straightened out in the darkness as well as conditions would permit, and firing parties were thrown forward to the crest of the ridge. The busy hum of many tongues, all intent upon relating the adventures of this nocturnal visitation, sounded strangely upon the crisp midnight air.

Confusion gradually subsided; every endeavor was made to ascertain our losses in men, horses, etc. Companies were sent out, after being formed. The horses could only be saddled in the darkness by one man holding his struggling and thoroughly terror-stricken brute, while another man adjusted the saddle and bridled him (no easy task), and until the gray of morning a sharp watch was kept to guard against another stampede.

It was ascertained that about seventy of our best horses and mules were gone, this loss falling principally upon "G" and "K" troops, as the Indians struck their flank first. It is doubtful if either of these troops had any "sleeping parties" among their herds. General Mackenzie lost a fine gray pacer, which he prized very highly, and his adjutant, Lieutenant Lynch, also lost a very valuable horse. The Comanches went almost over headquarters, as it was located directly under the ridge along which they rode, and where they first struck it.

When the alarm was first given, the writer frantically grabbed for his picket pin, only to see it whizzing through the air into the darkness beyond his reach, and his horse going like mad for the huddled herd of "F" troop. Following with desperate energy, knowing full well the value of his efforts in that direction, he saw the lariat catch in another; the horse jerked back; it held. His hand was upon it. He drew in hand over hand, upon the terrified animal. *He felt that he had drawn a prize.* The din and uproar was at its height. Getting a half hitch on his horse's nose and holding on with main strength, it was found that his hobbles—a new pair—were unbroken, and as soon as the tumult had somewhat subsided, the writer mounted him as speedily as possible and unattended—for it was impossible to find a trumpeter—started to ascertain what damage the picket posts had sustained. They had been overrun. The nearest post was about twenty yards outside of "F" troop's horses, and in charge of a Dutch corporal, who told his story in a very broken, brief, but ludicrous manner: "I vas lying down, sir, ven I hears a shot. I shoomps up, dries to get my bicket pin as de horses roosh py, and de next ding I knows de Injuns dey ride all ofer me. I raise my carbine to my preast as he broosh py me; he stagger, almost fall, and he deesappear in de dark."

The Stampeded Horses—Attack and Chase

While the command was still saddling up, and before the dawn was beginning to streak the east, I rode out through the gloom and sage brush to the other picket posts, crossed the Fresh Fork up to the saddle girth, pistol in one hand, bridle rein in the other, feeling at any moment that the Qua-ha-das might be on the outskirts of the camp to pick up loose horses. I saw the trail of the stampeded horses, but neither saw nor heard anything else until the last picket post on the bluff was reached. Their story was soon told, and the direction of the frightened horses going out. Cautioning them to give the alarm promptly, I passed on. Reaching the most remote post on the hill overlooking our camp, to gain which the river had to be recrossed, I was about to question the pickets, when I heard a shot (this shot was fired by Quartermaster Sergeant Morgan of "C troop), followed by a loud shout in the valley beyond. I galloped rapidly up. Here, coming from different directions, also at a gallop, I met two detachments of "K" and "G" troops which had been sent out shortly before to hunt up stray horses, and to find the trail of the stampeded herds. They were commanded by Captain E. M. Heyl and Lieutenant W. C. Hemphill. All looked down the valley. A dozen or more Indians were seen rapidly making off with as many of our horses. In a moment we were dashing after them. Although still quite dark their forms were distinctly visible. The men scattered out somewhat in the chase, the best and freshest horses of "K" troop leading. We gained on them rapidly, were almost within pistol shot, and a moment later the men began to open fire, when suddenly the Indians abandoned the animals and disappeared in a ravine or arroya, crossed it, and rode out on high ground beyond, toward a high bluff or mountain, now clearly outlined in the quickening dawn of day. Most of the men stopped short at the break or arroya, as there was an abrupt shelf or jump-off, quite difficult for any but the best horses to clear, but Captain Heyl and myself were close upon the Indians. We gave our horses the spurs, jumped the ledge into the ravine, scrambled out, and were again closely following them to the open prairie, now gradually ascending until it seemed to terminate in a smooth prairie ridge as we approached the mountain or butte.

Mount Blanco—"My God, We Are In a Nest!"

We were now more than two miles from the camp in a direct line, and more than that by the route we had come. As we ascended the ridge, glancing quickly to the front, there at the base of the bluff or butte could be seen in the clear light of approaching day the ground fairly swarming with Indians, all mounted and galloping toward us with whoops and blood-curdling yells that, for the moment, seemed to take the breath completely from our bodies. But a scant dozen of our men had followed us across that difficult arroya in the prairie, and the first, almost paralyzing, effect it had upon that little party can never be effaced from one's memory. The picture is indelibly stamped upon the brain.

It was like an electric shock. All seemed to realize the deadly peril of the situation and to take it in at a glance. For a moment the blood seemed fairly congealed, for we realized what the ruse of the Indians had been and knew now that their purpose had been to lead us into an ambuscade. We all drew rein on the ridge as one man, each looked at the other, and then raised a simultaneous sound of surprise. Captain Heyl was the first to speak: "Heavens, but we are in a nest! Just look at the Indians!" Although I echoed this sentiment, in my heart I could not speak it. No words could express it. No act could convey what we felt at that moment.

mence their curious custom of circling. They were naked to the waist; were arrayed in all their war paint and trinkets, with head dresses or war bonnets of fur or feathers fantastically ornamented. Their ponies, especially the white, cream, dun, and claybanks, were striped and otherwise artistically painted and decorated with gaudy stripes of flannel and colored calico. Bells were jingling, feathers waving, and with jubilant, discordant yells that would have put to blush any Confederate brigade of the Civil War, and uttering taunting shouts, they pressed on to what they surely considered to be their legitimate prey. Mingled with the shouts, whoops, and yells of the warriors could be distinctly heard the strident screeching and higher-keyed piercing screams of the squaws, far in rear of the moving circles, which rose above the general din and hub-bub now rending the air. In the midst of the circling ponies we could see what appeared to be two standard bearers, but upon their nearer approach we discovered them to be two scalp poles gaily decorated with long scalp locks, probably of women, with feathers and pieces of bright metal attached which flashed in the morning light. There were also other flashes seen along their line which I afterwards ascertained were small pieces of mirrors held in the hand and used as signals in the alternate advances and retreats, deployments and concentrations, in place of tactical commands. These were carried by the principal warriors or sub-chiefs, acting, I supposed, as file closers, squad leaders, etc. They had no squad, platoon, or company line formations, and no two, three, or four Indians were seen at any time to come together or bunch. While a general line was maintained at all times, it was always a line of circling, individual warriors with varying radii, expanding and contracting into longer or shorter lines, advancing or retreating during these tactical maneuvers. The scalp-pole bearers I took to be chiefs, or big medicine men, for they were arrayed in all the gorgeous trappings that savage barbarity is capable of displaying. It was a most terrifying spectacle to our little band, yet wild, grand, and novel (to look back upon) in the extreme. No shouts or cheers from our men were given in response to the diabolical yelling and din of screeches of the Indians. They maintained a stolid, grim silence, one of determination to do or die to the last. Unfortunately Heyl's men were nearly all new recruits who had just joined us on this expedition. They had never been in a fight before; were all well mounted on comparatively fresh horses, and as with him (Heyl), who was mounted, as has been already stated, on a large, powerful, black horse, full of fine spirit and strength, the excitement of the chase having partially subsided, everything thus far having gone their way, their fighting ardor had as rapidly cooled, and, seeing the ultimatum of being surrounded and massacred, unless assistance arrived very soon, chose to trust to their horses' heels in an endeavor to escape, rather than to face longer the ferocious Qua-ha-das, whose wild yells, whoops, screams, and screeches now sounded so unpleasantly close to their ears.

This is just precisely what they did do. To my utter surprise and consternation, on my attention being called by one of my men—"Lieutenant, look over there, quick; they are running out!"—I saw

Captain Heyl and his men "bunch," and with spurs in their horses' flanks, ride out of the fight at full speed.

Shouts, commands, threats, curses were of no avail. The moral effect of that wild, fancifully dressed, shrieking band of half-naked Comanches, drawing about our flanks and now beginning to close in with their arrows and pistols, was too much for raw men who had never been "tried out" under fire. To my utter dismay I was left a long distance in rear with these five men of "G" troop, a gallant, brave squad of men. We were still some hundreds of yards from the ravine toward which we had been slowly but gradually drawing when we first realized our critical dilemma. This was all done without any notice or warning being given to me by Captain Heyl. He had given no orders or instructions since we had first arrived on the ground.

At this movement by Heyl and his men, the Comanches gave an extra yell of supreme satisfaction, began bunching for a charge, and, making a sudden dash at us with some of the leading warriors, the bullets and arrows began coming in quickly, and to brush uncomfortably near us from every direction.

Knowing that it would be certain death should he turn, try to join the panic-stricken, retreating party, and make a run for the shelter of the arroya, the writer mounted his men, cautioned them to keep well deployed, cut off the magazines of their Spencer carbines, reserving them until the last moment, to commence falling back—using single shots—turning to fire, but on no account to turn and run until they got the word. The order was carried out to the letter. The Indians were poorly armed with muzzle-loading rifles and pistols and bows. We commenced moving to the rear, bending low on our horses, several of which were struck with arrows. We faced about as often as possible to fire and check them, hoping every moment to see the head of Mackenzie's column come out of the adjacent valley of the Fresh Fork. When we finally faced the leading warriors, a bullet struck Downey in the hand, cutting two fingers, as he was in the act of working the lever of his carbine. With his hand streaming blood, his efforts seemed useless. The shell would not eject. "Lieutenant, what shall I do?" I shouted, "Use your hunting knife, and eject the shell with it!" The brave man did it with his wounded hand, and firing a moment later, almost in their faces, dropped an Indian out of the saddle. They were still afraid of our carbines. Using them up to the last moment as single shooters, I shouted, as we neared the arroya: "Now unlock your magazines, bunch your shots, pump it into them, and make a dash for your lives! It is all we can do!" The Indians recoiled as we delivered this volley, and several going off their ponies caused some confusion, as we made the run. Thank God for those Spencers! My affection for them has never changed. It was not necessary that they should carry one thousand or twelve hundred yards, but kill at from five hundred down to twenty or thirty yards, in what almost became a mix-up. The situation had been desperate from the first. It now seemed to be absolutely hopeless. I never expected we would reach the arroya. I felt that our time to die had come, and many thoughts rushed unbidden to the mind. Gregg was about ten or fifteen yards to my right and rear, after we gave them our magazines and turned, riding then on my right flank. He said: "Lieutenant, my horse is giving out!" I glanced partly over my shoulder, and saw that it was too true. He was on an old flea-bitten gray, and the horse was beginning to sway in that peculiar manner always seen in an exhausted horse. The Comanches, almost by intuition, also knew that he was in their grasp, and the leading Indians, having partially recovered from the blizzard we had pumped into them, and seeing the animal stagger and falter, rushed in to dispatch the unfortunate man.

A large and powerfully built chief led the bunch, on a coal-black racing pony. Leaning forward upon his mane, his heels nervously working in the animal's side, with six-shooter poised in air, he seemed the incarnation of savage brutal joy. His face was smeared with war paint, which gave his features a satanic look. A large, cruel mouth added to his ferocious appearance. A full-length headdress or war bonnet of eagle's feathers, spreading out as he rode, and descending from his forehead, over head and back, to his pony's tail, almost swept the ground. Large brass hoops were in his ears; he was naked to his waist, wearing simply leggings, moccasins and a breech-clout. A necklace of bear's claws hung about his neck. His scalp lock was carefully braided in with otter fur, and tied with bright red flannel. His horse's bridle was profusely ornamented with bits of silver, and red flannel was also braided in his mane and tail, but, being black, he was not painted. Bells jingled as he rode at headlong speed, followed by the leading warriors, all eager to outstrip him in the race. It was Quanah, head war chief of the wild Qua-ha-das.

In vain did we try to save the life of the doomed man. I turned, checked up my horse, shouting for the men to do the same. With a Smith & Wesson pistol I fired several shots at a distance of not more than thirty feet, but the wily chief was on the other side of Gregg, and guiding his pony by rapid zigzagging so as to make a shield of him, his (Gregg's) life was in danger from our shots. Melville, at just this moment, was hit in the arm.

We dared not close with them, as that would, in a melée, be almost certain death. In vain did I shout for him to use his carbine. Alas! he did try, but, through nervous strain or excitement, his pull on the lever was too weak, and—the cartridge stuck.

Again I shouted, "Pull your six-shooter!" He reached for it. Too late! A flash! A report from the chief's pistol, now at Gregg's head—a fall—a thud—a tragic death—and his horse, now relieved of his rider, turned and ran into the Indian lines. *This was tragedy number one of Cañon Blanco.*

It seemed almost an age since we had first discovered the Indians, and they had charged out for us. But this had all occurred in a very brief space of time, much less than it has taken the writer to record it. It seemed as though General Mackenzie must have heard the firing and even then be coming out of the valley to our rescue.

Without stopping to scalp the fallen man or to finish us, as we naturally expected might now be done almost any moment, the Qua-ha-da suddenly whirled, and followed by his warriors—more than forty of whom were within a few yards of us—he rode rapidly toward the mountains.

We were saved! With a loss of one man killed and two men wounded, almost at the edge of the ravine, into which a few moments before the recruits of "K" troop had so ingloriously fled in a headlong demoralized flight.

The Gallant Act of Boehm—Our Rescue

What had proved our salvation? What had caused this sudden turning of the band? Did the wily chief suspect a decoy to the ravine, there to be met by the command, cut off, and his warriors massacred? Did he suddenly discover the dust of the column coming out of the adjacent valley by the Fresh Fork? Or did he consider his vengeance satisfied, blood for blood, for the warrior killed by the corporal at the picket post during the stampede?

A loud shout, and I turned quickly. Looking to my left in the direction toward our camp, I saw in a moment the true cause for our rescue, and the mysterious conduct of the now retreating Comanches. For, over the little hill or knoll which separated this prairie from the valley down which we had chased the Indians who were running off our stampeded horses, only in a shorter and more direct line to our camp, came all of our Ton-ka-way Indians, with Texas, the squaw, fantastically arrayed in all their finery, mounted on their war ponies, their carbines cracking, yelling with all their lungs, and kicking up such a dust that to the keen eyes of the wary Qua-ha-da chief indicated the rapid and close approach of the main column, which, coming up in his rear, would have pressed him between the ravine and the mountains, with a poor chance for escape.

Lieutenant Boehm had heard the firing; had rushed out in its direction; met the flying recruits, and, brandishing a carbine, compelled them to return, together with many stragglers from our chase belonging to the two troops; also Captain H—— and Lieutenant Hemphill, and, in another moment, waving on his "Tonks," the entire force, amounting now to not over forty men, but, with the heavy dust of a galloping column of over five hundred troopers close behind, were pressing the flying Comanches. Captain Heyl did not assume command, neither did Hemphill utter a word. Boehm said, "Bob, you take the left and I will take the right of the line! Let's push them now. Mackenzie is right in our rear." With our skirmish line well deployed we moved forward steadily toward the butte of the Cañon Blanco. A novel battle now ensued.

In the rear of the Indian lines could be seen the squaws now bringing up led ponies, keeping up their shrill, discordant screeching and screaming, and at the base of the butte, or low mountain, the savages were spread out, and circling here and there, looked like a swarm of angry bees, so that it was almost impossible to estimate the number of the moving mass with any accuracy, although we judged that there might have been from three hundred to four hundred—including the squaws.

They were heartily responding to the shouts and war whoops of our scouts, sometimes interladed with most emphatic and regular old-fashioned, round cursing. Here the real excitement and fascinating charm, so peculiar to an Indian fight, began. It was one grand, but rather dangerous, circus. As before stated, an irregular line of battle, or front, was kept up, always, however, in continual motion, every individual warrior fighting for himself—each, as he came around on the front arc of his circle, which he described with ever-varying radius, firing, whooping, or yelling, and brandishing his arms. This yell can hardly be described, but it approached a Yah-hoo! Y-a-a-h-h-0-0-0-0! and with the high keyed-up pitch.

At no time did our lines approach close rifle distance. Occasionally a Ton-ka-way would leave his circle, and, dashing straight to the front, would be imitated by a Comanche, both apparently bent upon meeting in personal combat, or a duel; but, as we breathlessly watched, expecting every moment to see the collision, they whirled, and delivering their fire, strongly reinforced by untranslatable Indian language—which we took to be serious name-calling—they darted back to their places in the ever-changing battle line.

This went on for some time. Occasionally a warrior could be seen to stagger as though about to fall; again, a pony was shot and fell, but instantly the wounded savage was hurried to the rear to be cared for by the squaws, who also brought up an extra pony, to remount the one whose animal had been shot, not forgetting to keep up their ear-splitting screaming, horrible screeching, and noisy exhibition of courage.

Upon the sides of the mountain, or high butte, the Indians could be seen gliding from rock to rock, and the puffs of smoke, from time to time, accompanied by the uncomfortable ping-p-i-n-g-g of the bullets close to our ears, told us that they had a lot of old target rifles in the hands of skillful marksmen on the summit. Their line was falling back rapidly, even before our small numbers. This was easily accounted for, as the dust of our main column was approaching nearer and nearer. The breaks or deep arroyas and numerous ravines in the prairie were full of Indians, hastening to the level ground beyond, to guard against surprise, there to keep up the rapid circling, firing, and falling back as before. They had no idea of being caught in any traps, and the rapid movement of the galloping column hastened their steps.

Charge Up the Butte—The Shattered Leg—Tragedy Number Two

Upon a suggestion to Boehm that we rout out the Indian sharpshooters from the butte, we took about a dozen men from the line and started up. Captain Heyl remained below. Our route was up the sides, and finally along a narrow, steep, zig-zag path, either a buffalo trail or one used by the Indians. We hardly knew but at any moment we might be picked off by a bullet. Urging my horse to his utmost speed by voice and spur to lessen their chance, I came suddenly upon a sharp, projecting boulder, jutting over the narrow trail. I turned my horse's head quickly, thinking to avoid it. Too late! Just at that moment he stepped upon either a rolling stone, or slipped and stumbled, and my left leg struck the boulder with a crash that almost sounded like the crack of a pistol, and I was almost lifted out of my saddle by its force. I grasped the pommel, for it made me sick, and all was dark and swimming before my blurred eyes. I felt myself sway and stagger, then apparently fall down an interminable distance. The cold sweat came from every pore, and I became unconscious, but dropped myself forward upon the horse's neck as I lurched. It has always been a puzzle how I got up the side of the butte. My horse had carried my dead weight, and my arms were still tightly clasped about his neck, with the reins loosely dangling. Luckily, the Indians, upon our nearing them, had hastily galloped off, abandoning the position, and scattering in every direction. I remember the cheering, seeing the big column come up, with

Mackenzie at its head, knew that we were saved—and then all is blank. The cool air at the top of the bluff, a dash of water in the face by one of the men, and a drink of water from his canteen revived me somewhat. The pain was intense, but, looking about me, I could see the Indians still falling back; could hear the cracking of the carbines, and shouts below, as the entire command deployed into lines and rode through the broken gullies and over the plain beyond. The Indians were being continually mounted on fresh horses, while our own were jaded and worn out by long and continuous marches, the stampede, and the hard run of the morning. I traversed the length of the butte slowly with my men and joined the column where it shelved off, it having arrived just in time to see the last Qua-ha-das rapidly disappear in the hills and bushy ravines that ascend to and clearly define the plateau of the "Staked Plains" or Llano Estacado. *This was tragedy number two of Cañon Blanco.*

Slowly we turned, further pursuit at that time being useless, and sadly retraced our march back over the ground just fought over to where the body of Gregg lay just as he had fallen when shot through the head by Quanah. We hastily buried him under the shadow of the butte (Mount Blanco) at its southeast foot, with the simplest form of a soldier's funeral, no chaplain being with us, and after heavy stones had been placed over the mound to protect it from the big wolves that swarmed all over this country, without unsaddling, we went into a temporary bivouac, and awaited further developments. Pickets were thrown out to guard against surprise, and the horses were allowed to graze under strong guard.

We remained here until about 2.30 p. m., the "Tonks" in the meantime coming in and reporting a broad and fresh trail leading up from the mouth of the cañon, which they said undoubtedly led to Quanah's village. Up to this time, in the excitement since the night before, I had neglected to attend to my wounded leg, but now that the nerves had somewhat relaxed, an intense pain warned me that, perhaps, it was more serious than I had supposed. It was now badly swollen and stiff, and growing more so. I called our contract doctor, A. A. Surgeon Rufus Choate, and consulted him. The boot had to be cut off. Slitting the boot leg down and removing all covering, it really presented a dreadful appearance. It was covered with clotted blood, black and blue, terribly swollen, with much laceration. The doctor, after a hasty examination, for the trumpeters were then sounding "boots and saddles," decided that the leg was not broken, but it might be a fracture, and considered it wise to put my leg in splints, which he did, using my boot leg and what material he happened to have on hand for that purpose. We had no ambulance or stretchers with the column, and there was no material at that place with which to construct a horse litter or a "travois," nor was there sufficient time. I mounted my horse; the command "Forward!" was given, and soon the column was moving around the base of the mountain and up the cañon to take the freshly discovered trail. It was impossible for me to go back forty miles of more to Lawton's supply camp on Duck Creek. Taking charge again of the pack train and rear guard, with instructions to afford whatever assistance to Lieutenant Vernou, now in command of the dismounted men, who had lost their horses, we moved out on the trail for the Comanche village.

The Pursuit—The Oua-ha-da Village and Ruse

These men were somewhat demoralized at the prospect of following afoot over many weary miles of plain, and through cañon, in search of our wily enemy, which had but a few moments before disappeared from our view on the horizon of the Staked Plains, and up the trail we were now on. A dismounted cavalry trooper is a much more demoralized man than a tired-out, straggling infantry soldier, since, from force of habit, he has learned to rely almost wholly upon the strength and brute courage of his faithful horse rather than in his own powers of endurance, thus subtracting to an important degree that factor of initiative so necessary in any soldier there in that country where our resources were so limited.

The saddles of our stampeded animals had all been concealed, or "cached," in some of the many small, bush-lined ravines, or "pockets," with which the country abounded. It was a hard march. Animals and men were very weary from the continuous strain of the previous forty-eight hours. By dint of hard talking, sharp commands, and even threats, accompanied by strong appeals to their pride, etc., we succeeded in getting the miscellaneous assemblage of foot-sore, chafed, blistered, mad, and disgruntled grumblers, grouchers and kickers, and the sore-backed horses and mules into camp, but it was at the expense of about every atom of our patience, strength, and nerves, and only after these "tag-ends" had all been urged and shamed into their last ounce of energy and patriotic ardor. We so informed Mackenzie that night. We bivouacked without shelter, "cross side lined" our animals, picketed the camp, and, with strong sleeping parties among the horse herds, we "turned in"—an almost exhausted command.

Mackenzie must have diligently chewed the matter over during the night (he rarely slept much anyway during an Indian campaign), regarding my plight, and the condition of these dismounted men, for early the next morning he sent for me. I was asked if I wanted to go ahead with the column, then moving out, or conduct these horseless troopers by slow and painful marches back to Duck Creek. He said, "I am told that your leg is badly injured, and the doctor has put your leg in splints. These dismounted men can go no farther with the column; they will only impede our march in pursuit. An officer will have to conduct them back, and this seems to be the only way in which you can, by taking charge of them, get good care and treatment at Lawton's camp. While it is true that I want you with me, I am looking out for your interest and safety. There is no ambulance with us to carry you should you become more disabled so that you can not march, and you had better go back. That is my advice and judgment." "Is it an order, sir?" "No, sir, it *is not* an order, but, I repeat, I am considering your comfort and safety." "Then, sir, if it is left to me, I go forward with the command!"

He added, "Another thing—I have been told that Captain Heyl did not behave well in that action yesterday morning. I had him transferred to this regiment because of his ability, efficiency, and reported gallantry in action. What do you care to say about it? You were a close witness of his conduct." I hesitated. At that period I could not feel like making any statement that would absolutely destroy the future reputation and permanent career of any officer who had stood sufficiently high in the estimation of Mackenzie to warrant his transfer to the Fourth Cavalry. So I quietly replied, "Well, General, if you have had him transferred on account of his previous good reputation as a gallant officer, I shall say nothing that might injure or destroy that reputation. I will merely say that under all of the circumstances of that affair, in my opinion he committed a *very grave error of judgment*, and you can draw your own conclusions!" He never took any action in the matter. I never referred to it again to him. Captain Heyl never made any statement, or spoke of it, either to Boehm or myself, and it passed into regimental "innocuous desuetude." Some time later, however, a most amazing event occurred—never fully solved—which caused all of the officers of the Fourth Cavalry who had full knowledge of the two tragedies already described to sit up and almost gasp with astonishment, as will be shortly shown.

In the National Cemetery of Arlington there is a memorial over Heyl's grave. On it is a full-length bronze tablet reciting most minutely the details of every event of his military career—*except that one incident.*

It is not recorded. He could never allow himself to figure or to be included in that tragedy—the death of Gregg, and my almost certain destruction in Cañon Blanco through that act. This is conclusive evidence that whatever Mackenzie, in his deliberations, decided to do or not to do, Heyl himself knew and felt what that act was, and that he could have no justification in perpetuating it in bronze at Arlington, unless he perjured his own soul or perpetrated a fraud upon the two men then living who were witnesses of that event. The writer left Mackenzie to draw his own conclusions forty-eight years ago. The reader can draw his own now in view of this omission on the bronze tablet. Many years after this affair, Captain Heyl told General H. W. Lawton, when both were Majors and Assistant Inspectors General: "Lawton, that day was the bluest moment of my military life. I was so dazed when I faced up to that horde of yelling, rushing Indians, with almost certain death staring me in the eye, that I simply lost my head and went in to a state of blue 'funk,' and the worst of it was, I could not help it! "This Lawton frankly told the writer, with no reservations of confidential secrecy, in the winter of 1888-9, while a guest for eight months in his house in Washington during that season.

Lieutenant C. A. Vernou went back with the dismounted men. The two columns separated, and were soon lost to sight as they moved in opposite directions. Everywhere, as we advanced up the cañon with its abrupt bluff faces, we saw evidences of its having been occupied by Indians, and scattered all along were many of the small "wickey-ups," still intact, put up for the use of the Indian herders, usually half-grown boys and girls. Every few miles the cañon widened out into more or less broad valleys bounded by almost impassable bluffs. We also saw numerous ravines and sand hills, as well as many small herds of buffalo. Here and there the creek (Catfish) widened out, sometimes presenting a succession of small, but beautiful, ponds or lagoons, clear as crystal, out of which swarmed immense flocks of wild ducks and curlew, and occasionally a majestic swan, whose trumpet notes sounded strange to our hunters who had rarely, if ever, seen such game. All the following day we marched steadily along, without catching even a glimpse of Indians, although they were undoubtedly spying on our every movement from their secret hiding places. The stillness and utter solitude of this lovely valley was only disturbed by the constant tramp of our horses' hoofs, until late in the afternoon when our trailers suddenly discovered the long sought for village, or where it had been—for what apparently was a large buffalo lodge village had suddenly vanished.

They had "folded their tents and silently stolen away," everything indicating a hasty departure. A broad lodge-pole and stock trail showed plainly out of the village, leading up the cañon. Our halt was brief, stopping only long enough to ascertain what was inside of the freshly heaped mounds of earth all about, which looked like small graves, and debris of every description. The "Tonks" laughed at this, and said it was done as a "blind" to detain us—to "pull wool over our eyes." Continuing, we soon came to where the trail divided; it was confused, crossing and recrossing in every direction, and for the first time our sharp-eyed scouts seemed "at fault." After much parleying and time lost, they concluded that the wily enemy had "doubled" on us and gone back upon the same trail. Countermarching and moving down the open valley again, we found, much to our chagrin, that it was even so, and after marching on the "back trail" until dark we were compelled to bivouac not far from where we had first discovered the abandoned village. The following morning, soon after we were in motion, the "Tonks" signalled from the edge of the bluff on the plains above us that they had "picked up" the lost trail leading over the seemingly impassable barrier. There was a long delay in scaling with horses the steep ascent, but, at length, after toiling over high, rocky bluffs and floundering around in the "breaks" and "arroyas," all were over and out of the cañon upon what appeared to be a vast, almost illimitable expanse of prairie. As far as the eye could reach, not a bush or tree, a twig or stone, not an object of any kind or a living thing, was in sight. It stretched out before us—one uninterrupted plain, only to be compared to the ocean in its vastness.

This was the beginning of the "Staked Plains," or "Llano Estacdo," which we had been seeking, and over which we would now be compelled to trail Quan-ah's moving village.

It was October 12, and a cold, overcast, gray morning. Our elevation was over three thousand feet. The air grew sharp and penetrating. We were all clothed for a summer campaign on the low plains of Texas. A severe "norther," peculiar to Texas at this season of the year, was beginning to strike us upon this barren waste, which, by contrast with the warm, bright sunshine of the previous day in the sheltered cañon, chilled us to the very marrow.

A short, dry, buffalo grass grew upon this immense plateau, over which our keenest-eyed "Tonk" trailers, now dismounted, were endeavoring to follow the slightest "signs." We moved along cautiously, marching slowly until about noon. Fresh signs of the Indian ponies in the large "caviard," or herd of horses which the enemy was driving, were the only indications of the course to be taken.

Lodge poles on the dry, stiff stubble gave no trail. Suddenly, however, the trail turned, and again went over the bluff into the cañon. This was unexpected; but, dismounting again, we led out "by file," slipping and sliding down the dangerous descent, until all were once more at the bottom, and again there was a confused lot of fresh trails—some leading up, others down, while still others led straight across the valley, directly at right angles.

Again, in our supreme disgust, we felt that we had been completely foiled. The "Tonks" scattered and rode rapidly all over the valley, and before the rear of the column had got fairly down into the cañon and closed up, they were waving us on. It had been found going out again over the bluff, this time, however, on the opposite side of the cañon. We were soon ascending for the second time that day the steep, precipitous sides of the rocky barriers. It was a singularly sharp trick, even for Indians, done, of course, to blind us and to gain time in moving their families of women and children as far as possible out of our reach. Without our own Indian scouts to beat the Comanches at their own native shrewdness, we would have undoubtedly lost the trail and hopelessly abandoned the task.

But now we found ourselves on a very broad and distinct lodge-pole and stock trail, leading in but one direction, and that to the west and northwest. We carefully estimated that they had from two to three thousand head of stock, and that the entire "outfit" was moving along with them, with all the plunder incident to a stampeding village. Could we overtake it, its capture was almost certain.

The "Norther"—"Hot Trail"—Night Attack—A Bitter Storm

The bitter cold increased, and on this high tableland, with no shelter, the wind from the northwest swept through our thin uniforms. Many had no overcoats or gloves, and the suffering grew intense. But we consoled ourselves with the though that if Indians with their women and children could endure it, we certainly must.

The trail grew fresher and "warmer." We now stretched out and moved more rapidly. We crossed numerous "carreta," or cart trails, made by the Mexicans in trading with the Comanches. They were well defined and headed toward the Pecos River. As we "rose" or "lifted" a slight ridge in the almost level prairie, we observed, in the far distance, moving figures, silhouetted against the sky line, as of mounted men galloping along the horizon, here as distinct as the sea line that limits the boundless ocean. First, two or three, then a dozen or more, until finally, on both sides of our now swiftly speeding column, there seemed to be hundreds. The "Tonks" said they were the Comanches, and we knew ourselves that at last we were on the right track! We now had them! Or, at least, we thought we did. Everybody was elated. The writer had not thought of his smashed leg, with its pain and uncomfortable splinter, for hours, so keen had become the excitement of this most absorbing chase, as the Comanches began to swarm on the right and left of the trail, like angry bees, circling here and there, in an effort to divert us from their women and children. Every preparation was made for a fight, for we firmly believed that, failing to throw us off the lodge-pole trail of their fleeing village, the red scoundrels had gathered all of their warriors for a determined resistance and a supreme effort should we overtake their families.

We knew that it is then that an Indian will fight with all the ferocity of a wild animal, blind to everything except the preservation of his squaws and pappooses.

Their efforts were therefore now all concentrated in an endeavor to throw us off the lodge-pole trail in order to gain time for the squaws. But Mackenzie determined, upon the advice of the Ton-ka-way chief and our best Indian campaigners, to disregard this wily bait, and keep steadily on, knowing that we must now be very close to them or the Qua-ha-das would not make such warlike demonstrations in the face of our superior force. We also fully realized that by keeping after the lodges, the warriors would soon close in and fight to the last Indian for the rescue of the ones they held most dear. Our object was, therefore, twofold. We could secure the ponies later.

The Qua-ha-das now began to get excited when it was found that we did not chase out after them, and, as we hoped, they began to swarm in toward us. The command was closed up in columns of fours, the men "counted off" again, and were directed to fill their blouse pockets with both carbine and pistol ammunition, of which we had taken along an ample supply. Cautionary commands were given for squadron and platoon formation, deployment to the front, right, and left, fighting on foot, etc. The pack mules, always a source of anxiety in the emergency of a battle, so far away from our base (nearly 100 miles), as they carried all of our precious food in this far-off wild, were closed in and placed in herd formation; a squadron was detached to surround them and guard them from stampede while still rapidly in motion—a sort of hollow square. A strong line of mounted skirmishers were thrown out to the front while flankers rode far out on the sides of the now threatening Comanches.

The Ton-ka-ways—McCord, the head chief; Simoon, "One-armed Charlie," Jesse, Lincoln, Grant, "Old Henry," Anderson, Job, William, Buffalo (the "Beau Brummer" of the "Tonks"), Black Bill, John Guy, and many others whose names can not now be recalled—slipped from their riding animals, caught up, from their pony herd being driven on the flank, their favorite war ponies, until then unused, stripped all superfluous loads from their saddles, and quickly began, in their rude, inartistic way, to paint and adorn their persons for the coming battle, which we now surely considered was impending. A small piece of looking glass, a puddle of saliva in the hollow of the hand, much red, green, yellow, and black paint (ochre), quickly applied in reeking daubs. The cream, claybank, dim or white pony was plentifully striped. Head dresses, horns, much red flannel, and bright-colored feathers completed the "Tonk" ensemble. The whole operation did not exceed five minutes, but sufficiently long to excite the laughter of the entire column of brave troopers even at that critical moment, when all were expecting a battle. Our gallant allies then pranced alongside the column, posturing, moving their heads from side to side, brandishing their carbines, and evidently feeling all the pride of conquering monarchs, so self-conscious were they of the dignity which all this display of paint, feathers, gew-gaws, etc., gave them.

The afternoon was now on the wane. We began to see ahead of us, although indistinctly, the dark, moving mass of the fleeing village. The Comanches still swarmed about our flanks. We came upon their fires, still burning, which they had hastily abandoned upon our approach. Then we struck a large lagoon of fresh water in a depression or "sink" in the prairie, where we hastily watered. Pushing rapidly on, we came upon lodge-poles scattered in large numbers on the trail in their sudden flight, also many iron and stone hammers, mortars, pestles, and all sorts of strange tools of the rudest description. Puppy dogs of the Indian half-wolf breed had been dropped by the squaws. The men picked up several and carried them on the pommels of their saddles. Great chunks of mulberry wood, and mesquite roots, used for cooking purposes when crossing this treeless desert, were also to be seen all along, and occasionally—what they never throw away unless hard pressed—the dried buffalo skins of their "teepee" or lodges. The chase had now grown "hot." The dark cloud of fleeing Indians loomed up closer. Still the Quaha-das dashed and circled about watching for a chance or vulnerable point for attack in our compact fighting column. Several times we thought that they were bunching for a charge, and our skirmishers and flankers grew more alert and drew in closer.

It grew darker and colder. The wind whistled. The air grew thicker and more hazy, and soon a cold rain, mingled with snow and sleet, began to drive into our faces, through our bodies, and into the very marrow. This was the supreme moment—a crisis. This was the time to have speeded up, made a sharp dash by a part of our command among the huddled, frightened, and demoralized women and children guarded for the most part only by old men and boys, while the other and larger half could have engaged and easily defeated the warriors. Nothing worse could have happened than a few men killed or wounded, but we surely would have got the entire "outfit," stock, women and children with all of their plunder, and made a "clean sweep up." Everybody was looking for Mackenzie to give the order to "Trot!" "Gallop!!" and "Charge!!!" It never came. This time he leaned, it seemed, on the side of extreme caution, and lost, what the writer believed at the moment, the best opportunity the Fourth Cavalry ever had for capturing practically Quan-ah's entire village and "lay-out." Or, it may be (for we never asked him the reason) that he was guided by feelings of humanity, and the big risk which we all ran, so far away from our supply camp, had our losses been heavy in a fight with a band that had always been noted for its bravery and hard-fighting qualities. Personally, it is the writer's belief that the snow and rain squall, driven by a howling northwest gale, was the determining factor that influenced, to a greater extent than any other, Mackenzie's judgment at that moment. Let us see what occurred. The village, which seemed but a mile or more away, was at once shut from our view, and to our utter dismay the inky blackness of night was instantly upon us. It seemed as though a great black curtain or pall had suddenly dropped in front of our eyes, shutting off every object. We could hardly distinguish forms about us even a foot or two away. Had the trot and gallop been taken half an hour earlier, there is little doubt that we would have captured the entire village and pony herd, but the menacing attitude of the warriors just as the storm was about to strike us, partly, if not wholly, diverted the General from his true objective.

The horses were very thin and much worn. We had no fresh mounts to draw from as the Indians possessed. The men were terribly fagged and tired; but the morale, *fighting spirit*, and *confidence was intact*, and all they needed at that moment was the word to "turn loose" and finish those Indians then and there—what they had come for, marched so many weary miles for, and sacrificed so much to accomplish.

Perhaps Mackenzie's judgment and wisdom was best, and we might have met with a calamity or dire disaster. "Quien Sabe!" But, looking back through that long vista of years it seems improbable, almost impossible, that we would not have achieved a complete success had we been given the command at the crucial moment before that black curtain fell and forever shut out the fleeing village and the "norther" that saved them. In discussing this campaign later, it was with the keenest regret and bitter disappointment that the driving of this half-breed Qua-ha-da into the Fort Sill reservation to become, later, a "good Indian" could not have been accomplished then by the Fourth Cavalry, instead of its being delayed until more than three years from that date, and then by converging columns operating in four different directions.

We were at once dismounted. Mackenzie seemed to be deliberating whether further pursuit was practicable, when the storm, which had been gathering all day and had already begun, burst upon us with renewed fury, cutting man and beast to the very vitals. It raged, sleeting and raining alternately, freezing as it fell and coating us with ice, which soon stiffened our clothes, and, as we could not see an arm's length before us, all hope of striking the trail was out of the question. The wind increased to a gale, and whistled and moaned incessantly. We formed a large ring, or defensive circle, with a radius of about one hundred and fifty yards, with the pack mules in the center. The men held their horses. While in this position, and awaiting further developments, a shot, then several, followed by a loud volley, greeted us, and the entire band of Comanches dashed almost over our close circle and instantly swept off into the impenetrable darkness that enveloped us, their taunting whoops and shrill yells sounding strangely to our gallant troopers as though to mock them in their helplessness. The Qua-ha-das had evidently seen the command halt before the storm broke upon us. The gloom of night had suddenly shut us from their view, and riding at breakneck speed in the direction where they had last seen us, to ascertain just our position, if possible, had accidentally stumbled upon us. All crouched down; the volley was returned; nobody was hurt, and the intense excitement this episode furnished us was soon over. Other difficulties confronted us.

A squadron under Captain Wirt Davis was hastily pushed out after their retreating forms, guided only by sound, and for a few moments the lurid flashes and loud banging of our skirmishers, rising high above the howling storm, indicated quite a lively fight, but, as the Indians fled, it soon ceased, and our men came in, having been lost at a distance of less than five hundred yards, and only guided back to the circle by a peculiar yell, rarely used by Indians except when lost, and now made by our scouts accompanying it and answered by those scouts who had been left inside the circle.

Every precaution was now made to shield men and horses from the piercing cold and the fury of the storm. Enormous hail stones had began to fall, pelting the animals so that they could only be held with the greatest difficulty, and bruising the men's bodies. "Tarpaulins" (canvas) were dragged from the mule packs; robes and blankets were fished out in the darkness and spread inside the circle, where they would do the most good, and keep all from perishing, and, half lying and squatting beneath these improvised shelters, we wore out the livelong night, one long remembered by every officer and man in that gallant command of the Fourth Cavalry. Pack mules and horses trampled, in their fright, near our heads and feet, and their continued moving and stamping, snorting, and wee-haw-ing made sleep out of the question among the men, who took turns by detail in holding on to the suffering animals. It was a bare existence, with nothing to eat since morning, and a bitter night to wear out. Mackenzie had no overcoat, and somebody wrapped his shivering form in a buffalo robe. Several wounds received during the Civil War had disabled and rendered him incapable of enduring such dreadful exposure.

It was with many misgivings that we thrust our heads out from under the close, heavy, lead-colored (painted) "paulins" in the sharp morning air. A beautiful day was ushered in. The frightful storm had spent itself, and was giving place to genial warmth and balmy sunshine. Without breakfast, we broke our "charmed circle," and, by early light, were soon on the trail, still plain and leading in the same general direction. There was little or no enthusiasm, however. The spirits of the column "flagged," for no living creature was in sight on that vast expanse. We knew, or felt, that the village had been moving all night, and it would prove a hopeless, stem chase—a long march, fruitless of results.

Soon a spy or two occasionally showed themselves on the horizon to watch our movements. A little later that wonderful phenomenon of the mirage was perfectly shown—

> "Clear shining through the swimming air,
> Across a stretch of summer skies."

The Return March—Dead Comanches—Mackenzie Wounded— Tragedy Number Three

Mackenzie soon found from our maps that in a direct west course the Pecos River was far away. The nearest post (Fort Sumner) was in New Mexico. The animals were now suffering for water, and some were beginning to show clearly signs of giving out. Our "chow" or rations were growing slim. The Comanches, by that lucky storm—for them— still had a night's march ahead of us, so he prudently, but most reluctantly, turned back.There was nothing to cook our food with but buffalo chips (bois de vache), and with scarcely water enough to wet our lips. We made a dry camp at our impromptu bivouac of the night before; the next day, in a sort of melancholy procession, reaching the lagoon, where it was decided to fill up with fresh rain water, and rest the command. The men on this day's march had picked up hundreds of smooth, well-worn cedar lodge-poles which the Comanches had dropped in their headlong flight, to be used for fuel at our bivouac supper. It was a most singular sight to see a long column of five hundred troopers, each with two or three fourteen-foot poles raised high in air over their shoulders. Mackenzie, who, at the head of the column, when his attention was first called to it, suspecting a joke, or that they were being carried along as relics, was about to seriously order them to be thrown away, when somebody suggested their possible utility for fuel instead of buffalo chips, which scented our bacon and coffee. They reminded one of a traveling circus, rather than a well drilled, disciplined body of cavalry.

The writer had been riding all this time with his battered leg in splints and closely bandaged. Upon Dr. Choate's inspection this day, after removing the bandages, it was found that it was not only not broken or even fractured, but was terribly bruised, and the flesh badly crushed and frightfully lacerated. Bathing it freely in the soft water of the lagoon, carefully cleansing and rebandaging it, I experienced little stiffness or pain. This lagoon we found to be full of countless numbers of curlew and many white swan, but none were killed.

Taking up the old route again the next day, there was absolutely nothing to relieve the voiceless march, so singular had become the effect of this mysterious silence of the Staked Plains upon the men. We leisurely dropped down again into Cañon Blanco, drinking in the quiet solitude and natural beauties of this Indian paradise. The "Tonks" were leading. The men and horses, who had been resting all day, now half asleep, were suddenly startled by the cry of "Indians! Indians!!" which brought every trooper erect in his saddle. All was soon organized activity. A healthy excitement ran through the bronzed column. Striking a trot, lope and gallop, all carefully closed up, and horses well in hand, we soon saw our advance scouts running at breakneck speed toward some small ravines, followed by the leading troop. The excitement grew intense. Two Comanches had been discovered following our old trail up the cañon, dismounted and leading their ponies. When discovered by our "Tonks" they abandoned their animals and ran into some bushy ravines, our scouts closely pursuing. As soon as we arrived, all entrances were closed. The "Tonks" went up over the bluff, thus cutting off their escape in that direction. Mackenzie directed the leading troop to open fire, while our Indians, by their fire from above, tried to drive them out into our command. The Comanches were game. They would not come out. Mackenzie ordered Boehm to take fifteen dismounted men and drive them out. There were several openings into the ravines. Boehm divided his men, and worked several paths. Mackenzie, becoming impatient, dismounted and got in behind Boehm to direct him, the two Comanches firing all the time. Just then something happened. A sharp swish, a thud, and a spiked arrow buried itself in the upper, fleshy part of Mackenzie's leg. He hurried back to the rear and had the spike cut out and the wound dressed. Soon all firing ceased, and we knew that the two Comanches were dead. The "Tonks" came down from their high perches on the bluff overhead, where they had given the entire command one of the finest circus acts (with several rings) of lofty tumbling, somersaults, vaulting, standing on their heads, etc., it had ever been our good fortune to see in an Indian country, and, upon parting the bushes, found both Qua-ha-das.

One was shot several times through the body, the other through the head. One had been shot in the hand while firing his pistol. The bullet had shattered the pistol butt. A bloody bow-string showed that he had used his bow later. With the strength necessary to draw the string, it must have proved very painful, and a clear test of the Indian's wonderful courage, tenacity, and stoical nature under certain circumstances. One of our men, a farrier of Troop "H," had been shot through the bowels, and, in tinning, was shot in the hand. *This was the third tragedy of Cañon Blanco.*

As it was getting late, we bivouacked near the spot. The "Tonks" entered the ravine, shot a few bullets into the Comanches' bodies, as was their custom, scalped them, ears and all, and then cut a small piece of skin from each breast, for good luck, or rather "good medicine"—such was the peculiar superstition of the Indian. This, dried in the sun, and placed in a bag, or attached to a string and worn next to the person of the warrior, acts as a safe guard against danger or sickness in any form. It was their "medicine" or "mascot." At night Dr. Rufus Choate, Lieutenant Wentz C. Miller, and two negro boys, field cooks, went up the ravine, decapitated the dead Qua-ha-das, and placing the heads in some gunny sacks, brought them back to be boiled out for future scientific knowledge.

The Boiling Heads—And Wounded Farrier

Shortly after midnight we heard the wolves, which had sniffed the flesh from afar in the keen night air, fighting, snarling, and howling like incarnate fiends over this horrible human feast.

A barbarous and tragical end to a barbarous band, who, while mutilating and heaping red-hot coals upon the nude forms of their writhing victims (as the writer had seen the preceding May at the massacre on Salt Creek prairie) in the peaceful settlements of Texas, dining their numerous blood-thirsty raids, had danced for joy at the savage torture inflicted.

Before starting the next morning, a horse litter had to be constructed upon which to carry our wounded man. The poles were lashed to the pack saddles of two mules traveling tandem. Cross-pieces were lashed to them in rear of the croup of one mule and in front of the breast of the other. A head covering was made of a framework of boughs, over which a blanket or shelter tent was thrown. He was thus carried one hundred miles, and by the personal nursing and unremitting attention of our faithful and efficient doctor, Rufus Choate, he lived, although his bowels had been perforated.

On this day we had but just gone into camp, and were about to eat our dinner, when Miller shouted to Major Mauck and myself, from a short distance up the cañon, "Come up, we have something good!" "What is it?" Miller replied, "soup!" We had observed two camp kettles strung on a pole over the fire. Seizing our cups, never suspecting a joke, we reached the spot. When to our horror we saw the two Comanche scalped heads, with the stripes of paint still on their faces, and with eyes partly opened, bobbing up and down, and rising above the mess kettles, mingled with the bubbling, bloody broth. It was a gruesome spectacle. With hands on our stomachs, we fled, directing "Bob," our valuable sable cook to transfer our dinner and all of our personal belongings farther down the cañon, out of sight and reach of our esteemed ethnological head-hunters and skull boilers. A more sickening sight it would be difficult to conceive of. We were no longer hungry that night.

There was a night alarm about midnight. Some Indians who had followed our trail tried to creep by our pickets, which, as officer-of-the-day, the writer had charge of, and stampede our horses. They were soon driven off with the assistance of "F" troop (Wirt Davis). We moved slowly down the cañon, the animals getting weaker and weaker. Lieutenant Warrington was sent in to Lawton's camp on Duck Creek to direct him (Lawton) to move his train and meet us at the Fresh Fork. Here we camped near the scene of our tragedy of October 10. Many of our hardships for the time being were forgotten in complete rest, good food, and calmness of mind and body. We visited the scene of our action. Armfulls of arrows were brought in, and all shuddered who had participated in the narrow escape, and loudly praised the prompt action and bravery of our noble, gallant "Peter" Boehm and the conduct of our faithful friends and rescurers, the Ton-ka-way scout allies. Upon going to Gregg's grave, it was found the earth had been dug up by wolves so that it was nearly uncovered. The region was scoured for larger stones with which to cover and anchor it down.

The wounded farrier of Troop "D" who had been shot through the bowels, and whom we had brought down the cañon on the horse litter, was very low. The ball had passed completely through him, cutting the intestines, which, with the fecal matter, exuded from the hole in his back. Gas was also being emitted from the wound. No one believed he could recover. Our efficient, tireless, ever-persevering A. A. Surgeon, Dr. Rufus Choate, never left him for a moment. He not only devoted his professional skill to saving the man's life, but, as a nurse, his tireless care and attention, notwithstanding the long period of jolting over very rough ground, placed him on the road to a quick recovery and permanent cure. He could only retain liquid food, nourishment taking place by absorption. It was Dr. Choate's object, therefore, to afford this with the least possible strain upon his physical and nervous system. Buffalo meat, devoid of all fat or gristle, was converted into a strong beef tea by quick methods. Liebig's condensed beef was added to this hot "bouillon," and poured into him as often as possible, at least without nauseating.

His wound thus closed, while his strength was conserved, and in this manner his life was saved. It was one of the most marvelous recoveries—due to perseverance, skill, and devotion to duty by an unselfish medical officer—known to us who had seen many deaths from culpable neglect both during the Civil War and afterwards. Two years later the writer saw this man, who had been discharged, working in the Quartermasters Corral at San Antonio, Texas.

"Camp Misery"—The Doctor's Practical Joke on Mackenzie

Several horses died here. Others, too weak to move, had to be shot, and still more were broken down. Lawton arrived with forage and rations for the horses and men. Mackenzie, feeling confident that Quanah, finding that on account of the storm we had abandoned further pursuit, would turn back from the Pecos River and move to one of their old, well-known haunts on Pease River, determined to send a part of the command in further search of him, taking command himself, sending all disabled, dismounted men, and weak, sick animals into Duck Creek. On October 24 the two commands separated. After reaching Duck Creek, Mackenzie's wound proved too painful and he was compelled to come in, and joined us on the 29th. From this camp we moved to another, in a frightful storm of rain and hail. The "pull" through the sand and "shin oak" killed off more animals. The General was irritable, irrascible, mean and "ornery." Nobody seemed to want to go near him even for sociability. Our esteemed A. A. Surgeon, Dr. Gregory, who had remained with the infantry at the supply camp, incubated a scheme or practical joke, however, which he confided to Lawton and the rest of us, by which he was going to "put one over" on the "old man." He would go and tell him that it was necessary for the preservation of his life for him to keep quiet and calm, etc. Otherwise he would be compelled to *amputate his leg*. He went to Mackenzie's tent. We watched him disappear. Shortly after we saw the doctor shoot out of the tent and make for his own, his face a deep scarlet. We could only guess at the result. We ascertained later, however, from him that with the conscious importance of professional skill, he took off the bandages, examined the wound, and with the utmost gravity told General Mackenzie that it was very much inflamed, and unless he controlled his irritability, he would be compelled to amputate the limb. He got as far as amputate when the General seized a crutch or big cane, and making for the doctor caused him to jump out from under the tent flap to save his own head from amputation. He did not repeat that advice. The joke fell flat.

From this camp the writer was directed to take command of all the dismounted and disabled men, sore-backed horses and mules, all the "tag ends," and proceed to Cottonwood Springs on the Double Mountain Fork, put them in camp and await the return of Major Mauck with his column from Pease River, while Lawton was ordered to take the supply train into Fort Griffin, load with half forage of corn, and return to our camp. This was carried out. The writer spent a lonely five days in the new camp. Thousands of buffalo darkened the prairie about us.

Besieged by Wolves—A Dose of Strychnine

Frequently on the march we came suddenly upon many packs of wolves of from eight to ten in number, dashing ahead of the column through the numerous breaks which cut our trail. They were hanging on the outskirts of the immense herds, waiting patiently for some young calf, or sick, or wounded buffalo left to die, which they soon feasted on. Many a bleached skull remote from the herds attested the untiring patience of these savage hangers-on to the interests of their ever-craving appetites. It was not so easy, however, to get the calves at all times, for the cow buffalo, unaided, was no weak fighter and defender of her young, and, when aided, as was generally the case, by a circle of young bulls, the cowardly sneak thieves were frequently tossed and trampled out of all shape. It was rarely the case, therefore, that a pack of wolves would go into a buffalo herd and made a desperate fight for a calf or a distressed cow. It was only when the helpless animals were abandoned that the wolves banqueted.

We gathered all the disabled animals and sick and wounded men, made a small enclosure, or breastwork, on three sides of a square, out of boxes, barrels, bags filled with earth, etc., pitched our tents, placed everything inside and prepared for a defensive stay—a period of "watchful waiting"—until the return of the Pease River column.

We had every reason to believe that the hostiles, eluding the column sent there, might seek and follow our trail with a large body; if so, our little handful of men would, it was feared, have made a feeble resistance if attacked. At night the wolves came out of the "bottoms" and numerous coulees, arroyas, and ravines, in countless numbers and besieged this camp. The sick and wounded became very nervous, for in their boldness the ravenous animals advanced to within a few feet of our tents in their eagerness for the meat which we had hung all about us in large quantities for immediate use, besides the carcasses scattered here and there had attracted their scent, and in the glare of the campfire their long, white teeth could be distinctly seen, as they tumbled, fought, and howled over their canine feast. It came as an unpleasant episode in our enforced imprisonment. No such number of wolves had ever been seen or heard by us in that country. If some came nearer than others, we charged them with large fire brands, throwing them in their midst, whereupon the brutes scattered in every direction. They dreaded fire. About the third or fourth night, however, during which it had been impossible to sleep, their number seemed to increase and double up. They became bolder than ever, for now, outside the camp, they had but a few bones to quarrel over, having picked them white, while our fresh meat was still a very great temptation. The little A. A. Surgeon, Dr. Culver, who had been with the infantry column, and Lieutenant Speer of the Eleventh Infantry, became perceptibly nervous, if not actually alarmed. We played cards to divert our minds, but still the wolves gathered and crowded in upon us. We did not dare to open a rifle fire upon them for fear our shots might attract any Indian scouts that might, perhaps, be lurking about our trail.

The doctor had a quantity of strychnine among his medical stores, and, at the suggestion of the writer, we used it all in poisoning a quantity of meat and scattering it here and there. We soon had the satisfaction of hearing their blood-curdling yells and howls while fighting for the poison. When morning came, we found them stretched out in every direction; some were dead, others were *wanting to die*, being in their last agonies after having gone to the stream to "water up," where we found their already bloated bodies. It was only a temporary cessation of hostilities. On the last night, not daring to sacrifice any more of our meat, which we might need, for we had no serviceable horses with which to run the buffalo, still in large numbers all about us, we tried the experiment of poisoning some of the wolf meat. They again congregated by thousands, coming out of the river bottom at dusk and remaining until the first streak of dawn. They sat upon the bluffs, gathered about the carcases, and again set up noises hideous enough to cause the hair to stand upon end, but they would not touch the meat. They will not banquet upon their own kind unless driven to it by desperation, no matter how much the meat might be disguised. This lobo fraternity had been pretty well fed up. Again we could get no sleep, and once more resorted to firebrands. If one could control their nerves, the tumbling and stampeding of this vast throng would have been most laughable. But their terrifying yells had somewhat the same effect upon the doctor and Lieutenant Speer as the Germans in their campaign of frightfulness in the world's war. The more noise, the greater the effect. The writer had heard this noisy yelling in many battles of the Civil War. Thus we spent five days and nights in this wolf-besieged camp, with nothing to do, and nothing to see but that vast expanse of solitude and wilderness, the horizon of which was a constant mirage, except the immense buffalo herds which we could no longer reach except by still-hunting.

The March In—Snow, Sleet, Abandoned Animals—"Home Again!"

On November 6, the command from Pease River under Major Mauck arrived in the midst of a dense, driving snow storm and "norther," it having snowed the night before to the depth of five inches and grown colder, and many animals had died at the picket line, their backs crusted with snow and ice. Many of his command were riding pack mules. They had been unsuccessful in their search for the Comanches. The animals, many of them, were mere shadows. They needed some com for feed and fuel so that we might save those that remained and get them in by short and slow marches. Lawton rolled in the next morning (8th) with his corn train. Both outfits had had a rough time. We commenced to feed full forage. The poor brutes could hardly stand up. With great caution, and amidst intense cold and much suffering among men and animals, we made our may in across California and Paint Creeks and the Clear Fork of the Brazos, and slowly into Fort Griffin, which we reached on November 12, singing the same old song with which we had started more than a month before: "Come home, John, don't stay long; come home soon to your own Mary Ann!"

The writer left thirty wolf skins under five inches of snow in that wolf camp on the Double Mountain Fork—enough to make eight large, fine robes—which he never saw again.

On the night of the 13th the "Tonks" gave us a scalp dance in their village on the flat below the post. They had divided the two scalps into 8 equal parts. We did not stay long. It proved to be too warm in their small "tepees," and too "smelly," as they had stripped off in the dance down to their breech clouts, and later, when they discarded them, *was the time when we departed.*

On the 17th we were slowly marching across Salt Creek prairie toward Fort Richardson; when about halfway across, near the scene of the massacre in May, a storm of rain and sleet, which had been brewing all day, broke upon us. It blew a gale and toward night had changed to a driving sleet, hail, and snow storm, compelling us to go into camp. The men were much exposed all night trying to save the animals from perishing by using their saddle blankets for covers. Many died, however, during the night, and more men were mounted on the pack mules. Major Mauck, who was in command, decided, if we were to save the remainder, we must make a desperate effort to negotiate the remaining twenty miles, and that without delay. Breaking camp early, therefore, in the midst of the raging storm, the snow from six to eight inches deep, we "led out," the men dismounted, and the entire command floundered and staggered into the protection of the post-oak timber near Rock Station, fourteen miles from Fort Richardson, where we were somewhat sheltered from the pitiless hail and sleet which cut our faces like glass, and, after a short halt, pushed on, arriving at the post at three p. m., tired out, cold, hungry, and dirty. We had at last arrived "home," for that was what it seemed to us, after most of the regiment had been in the field since May 1. All were delighted to greet their wanderers, and, like all soldiers' hardships and sacrifices, they were all soon forgotten in hot baths, change of clothing, good grub, complete rest, and the warm congratulations of our friends and the love of anxious, devoted wives and families.

Mackenzie's Amazing Report—The Fourth Cavalry's Verdict

Owing to the writer's hesitation and unwillingness to characterize Heyl's conduct, place it in its proper light, or to reflect in any way upon his conduct as an officer, because of Mackenzie's strongly avowed personal liking and attachment for him, together with the statement he made to me on the morning of October 11 in Cañon Blanco when about to send back the dismounted men to Duck Creek, as to his reasons for desiring Heyl's transfer from the Ninth to the Fourth Cavalry, and my sudden resolve, in view of such frank reasons, to say or do nothing to blast that officer's reputation among his brother officers in the regiment, or at that time in the Army, a most amazing event occurred which, in its far-reaching effects, caused the officers of the Fourth Cavalry, who had full knowledge of the two tragedies already described to sit up and almost gasp with astonishment. Mackenzie made a report! The reaction which followed such a report is difficult to contemplate or clearly analyze even after the lapse of nearly half a century. They were simply confounded. It was then and will always be most difficult to explain, except upon the fact, which developed later, that he was even at that period, already showing unmistakable indications of dementia or mental aberration.

Mackenzie came in from that campaign a sick and very much disappointed man. Circumstances, entirely beyond his control, worked against his entire success, as he had so optimistically hoped for. He was, therefore, incapable, or in no condition, to make a clear, concise, and dispassionate report of this affair in the Texas panhandle. This is clearly shown, not only by his inaccurate statements, some of the days of movement even being wrong, but it is a mere skeleton. By this report it will be seen that no mention whatever had been made either of Boehm's generous and gallant act or of the writer and his almost fatal injury. *We were both absolutely ignored.* It will also be observed that he does not even report himself as wounded, but that he returned "on account of sickness." The officers were all amazed that he made no such mention, when it was so well known, even among the men, that Heyl and Hemphill figured only in a most unfortunate incident, since no orders were given by either of them at any time, except his (Heyl's) order to "mount" and "run out." Boehm and myself, besides the few men with us, were the only witnesses of that act, and had a full report been called from either of us, his (Heyl's) hopes would have been blasted forever. The writer saw Boehm and his Ton-ka-way Indian scouts, with other men whom he had gathered in his gallant run to my rescue, driving Heyl and his panic-stricken men back to our line at the point of his (Boehm's) carbine.

Mackenzie's report follows. In no sense does it cover the scope or period of our active operations, and but few, if any, of the important, vital details or recurring incidents of the campaign, and is otherwise incomplete in every respect as well as badly misleading. As a report it was absolutely valueless. It could not have been taken from any note book, itinerary, diary or memorandum of any kind, because the initial dates are wrong. It shows an absolute lapse of memory.

HEADQUARTERS,

Fort Richardson, Texas, November 17, 1871.

THE ASSISTANT ADJUTANT GENERAL,

Department of Texas.

Sir:

I have the honor to state that I reached this post on the 8th instant, having been obliged to leave the command on the 28th of September (?), en route to the head of Pease River, on account of sickness.

A part of the command had a skirmish with the Indians on the 11th of September (?) (Note—We left Camp Cooper October 3) near the Freshwater Fork of the Brazos River, in which one soldier was killed, the loss of the Indians, if any, not being known.

The Indians were followed until the 14th, when the trail was left at a point about forty miles west of the Freshwater Fork of the Brazos, and supposed by me to be about eighty miles east of Fort Sumner, New Mexico. Returning, two Indians were killed near the Fresh Fork of the Brazos, one soldier was wounded. A very bad stampede was effected by the Indians on the hills near our camp—firing, etc. This took place on the night of the 10th (?), and by it sixty-five horses were lost. This interfered very much with subsequent movements. A full report with map and itinerary will be sent as soon as the command returns.

I have the honor to be.

Very respectfully, your obedient servant,

(Signed) RANALD S. MACKENZIE,

Colonel Fourth U. S. Cavalry.

Official copy.

(Signed) H. CLAY WOOD,

    Assistant Adjutant General.

No further report could ever be found at Headquarters, Department of Texas.

                      HEADQUARTERS,

            Fort Richardson, Texas, February 5, 1872.

THE ASSISTANT ADJUTANT GENERAL,

    Department of Texas,

    San Antonio, Texas.

SIR:

I have the honor to transmit herewith maps of two scouts under my direction during the past year, one to the headwaters of the North Fork of the Red River, and one to the head of the Freshwater Fork of the Brazos. * * *

Very respectfully, your obedient servant,

            (Signed) R. S. MACKENZIE,

        Colonel Fourth Cavalry, Commanding Post.

Itinerary of scout of Companies A, B, D, F, G, H, K, and L, of the Fourth Cavalry, and Companies F and I, Eleventh Infantry; Colonel Ranald S. Mackenzie, Fourth Cavalry, commanding:

From October 3 to October 10, 1871, marched (west by northwest) one hundred and forty-six miles, camped on Freshwater Fork of the Brazos.

October 11, 1871, about 1 a. m., Indians attacked the camp. The horses were frightened and sixty-six stampeded. At daylight the command was ordered to saddle up. Shortly afterwards, a small party of Indians were seen off on the hills, when Captain Heyl with a small portion of Company K, and Lieutenant Hemphill with a detachment of Company G, gave chase. After running the Indians for two or three miles they came upon a very large party of them; had a skirmish in which one man of Company G was killed. The command chased the Indians about eight miles, but could not get near enough to engage them. The Indians scattered and went off in small parties. Captain Heyl and Lieutenant Hemphill together had about fifteen men. Found large Indian trail and marched on it north by northwest fifteen miles, and camped on some ponds on the Freshwater Fork of the Brazos. October 12, 1871, marched north by northwest and camped on the river. October 13, 1871, marched twenty-one miles west by north, and camped on Staked Plains. Saw several parties of Indians, but could not get near them. Several attempts were made to overtake them. About seven p. m. one of the pickets reported a large body of Indians preparing to charge the camp, when two or three companies were ordered out to meet them. Upon arriving at the ground where the Indians were seen, it was quite dark. The Indians fired several pistol shots and then went off. Nothing more was seen of them.

October 14, 1871, marched eighteen miles (west); found Indian trail so scattered that it was impossible to follow it farther. The command turned around and marched twelve miles east. October 15 and 16, 1871, marched thirty-six miles east by south. October 17, 1871, marched nine miles (east by south) when two Indians were seen in the valley of the river. They were pursued and killed. One man of Company H was wounded in the skirmish. October 18 to November 8, 1871, marched two hundred and forty-seven miles (east by northeast) and arrived at Fort Richardson, Texas.

(Signature not included in copy.)

Official extract and copy.

(Signed) J. B. MARTIN,

Assistant Adjutant General,

While it is not charged that he (Heyl) was directly responsible for the injury which the writer sustained on that morning, because he did not cause his horse to fall, nor did he place the boulder on the buffalo trail against which the leg was smashed, it is, nevertheless, just as certain that he was indirectly responsible, from the fact that, as the ranking officer of the other two, who had placed themselves under his command just as soon as they had joined the chase, he led them into an ambuscade or trap which the Indians had prepared for us, and which by the freshness and speed of his horse and those of his men enabled him to do, and then, when he found that we were all liable to be cut off and massacred, by that same agency or resource, and with the full responsibility of command upon him, he not only did not exercise his authority as commanding officer, or give us any warning, but, finding that he could save himself and the lives of his men by fresh and fleet horses, he ran out and left us to be sacrificed.

This was the first Indian action in which the writer had been engaged, and he naturally looked to one who had been a captain of volunteer cavalry, and a captain of a regiment with such a reputation as the Ninth United States Cavalry then had, and who had come to our regiment upon Mackenzie's recommendation, for guidance and decisive action.

Fighting Spirit and Efficiency vs. Criminal Neglect—Capture, Mutiny, and Fighting Paralysis

During the Civil War, Heyl had been an officer of the Third Pennsylvania Volunteer Cavalry. On November 28, 1862, that regiment was posted at the most vital point in the outer picket line of the Army of the Potomac, one squadron, with a picket outpost and its reserve, being near Hartwood Church, Virginia, under a Captain George Johnson. Heyl was in this command. They had been specially warned and directed to remain saddled up during tile night and to exercise more than the usual precautions, as an attack was expected in force that morning. At sunrise a picked column of Stuart's Confederate Cavalry completely surprised this picket outfit, overran it, and captured the entire body, with all of their horses and arms, except five outposts who escaped into the woods, but left their horses. No fight seems to have been "put up." There were captured, according to Confederate reports, eighty-seven men, two captains, three lieutenants, two colors, one hundred horses, carbines, etc. It was one of the most shameful and humiliating affairs that every occurred in the history of that war. General Hooker characterized it as "a disgraceful affair," and called a court of inquiry "to fix the responsibility upon the culpable, and have them brought to trial and punishment." The "greatest vigilance and care" was enjoined upon this command. General Averill, the Division Commander, in commenting upon it, said, "He permitted his command to be surprised and a great portion of it captured, bringing disgrace and shame upon his regiment and the brigade to which it belonged, and our cavalry service into disrepute," and he requested that Johnson be dropped from the rolls! By order of the President he was "summarily dismissed." Captain Johnson was, of course, as ranking officer, and therefore responsible, made the scapegoat. But the other officers were also equally culpable. Heyl was either with the picket outpost, or with the reserve, and was captured in this shameful manner. That fact alone probably saved him from the same fate as Johnson. Such a surprise in time of war, at the most vital point in our lines, and wholesale capture and "sweep up" of a cavalry picket supposed to be guarding the safety of the Army, could only have been the result of the culpable carelessness and criminal neglect of the five officers, including Heyl, who were captured with all of their men, and without apparently much resistance, four men only being wounded, with no loss to the enemy. It was a subject for comment by Generals Lee and Wade Hampton. Had Stuart been backed up by a large force of infantry, it would have afforded Lee an opportunity, which he had not before enjoyed, to have seriously menaced the entire Union Army. Heyl told the writer that he had been a prisoner during the Civil War, but he never related the details. These can be found with a circumstantial narrative, correspondence, etc., in the Rebellion Records, Volume 21, Series 1, pages 13-17. There is no other instance known in the history of the Civil War where a squadron of cavalry on outpost picket duty was surprised and absolutely overrun and captured in a body through the criminal neglect and cowardice of its officers.

Heyl was appointed a first lieutenant. Ninth Cavalry, July 23, 1866, and captain July 21, 1867.

About 1868 or 1869 he was in command of a troop of that regiment, and in camp near San Antonio, Texas. A mutiny broke out among his men. He shot his first sergeant dead. It was all *he* could do. A court of inquiry exonerated him for the act. It was all *they* could do. But, the query in the Army always was: Why this mutiny if the discipline in that troop, or the loyalty of his men for him, was what it should have been?

Let us stop to ponder for a moment.

Here we have cited three disgraceful affairs in which Heyl had prominently figured or been involved during a certain period of his military career:

I. The disgraceful and shameful picket affair of the Third Pennsylvania Cavalry near Hartwood Church, Virginia, by which, through his own culpable neglect or criminal carelessness, he was taken prisoner.

II. The unnecessary killing of the First Sergeant of his troop near San Antonio, Texas, of which, although it is true he was exonerated, there is almost always a suggestion, if not conclusive evidence, that a mutiny is generally caused by harsh treatment and brutality, or criminal neglect of the true interests of one's men. In nearly every such instance during the Civil War it was found to be true.

III. Rank, white-livered cowardice in the affair with Quan-ah Parker's band of Indians, when he became panic stricken, showed the "white feather," and ran out of the fight, leaving his comrades to be killed. And yet he "carried on," being appointed, either through political pull. War Department favoritism, or theatrical self-advertising, in the Inspector General's Corps, gaining one promotion after another until he attained the grade of Colonel and Assistant Inspector General at the time of his death.

Commendatory Letters Confirm Statement

Following are letters from the late Major (then Lieutenant) P. M. Boehm, the late Major (then Lieutenant) W. A. Thompson, the late Lieutenant, Colonel (then Captain) John A. Wilcox, and others, voluntarily given in support of the writer's statement:

Boehm says: "I was present at the time the Indians made the charge, and I can vouch for the brave conduct and skill of Lieutenant Carter. I can not express in too great a sense the ability shown by this officer in covering the retreat, and holding his men in such a position as held the Indians back."

Thompson says: "Had it not been for your coolness, good judgment, and great gallantry that morning, the chances are ten to one the whole command would have been killed before we could have reached them. * * * *Prompt and decisive action and bravery held the men to their work and saved the day.* * * * The Qua-ha-da Indians are noted for their great bravery and close fighting. I can add that the part taken in this Indian fight by Captain Heyl (late Fourth Cavalry) left the impression that all the credit was due solely to Captain P. M. Boehm and Lieutenant R. G. Carter (at which time both were Lieutenants of Fourth Cavalry, now retired."

Wilcox says: "Your personal bravery in the fight near the Brazos River when the Indians partially cut off your little detachment, and killed your sergeant, is well known to all the old officers of the Fourth Cavalry. In regard to the occurrences incident to the fight at Remolino,

Mexico. I was present and distinctly recollect your coming up and reporting that you had but recently killed an Indian. I am familiar with your statement about the packs being cut loose from the mules. * * * I distinctly recollect the 'captured Indian' you speak of being brought into camp by the Seminole scout; his efforts to shoot Captain Mauck and his being killed on the spot. Many discharged their pieces, and you among the rest. I was standing within ten steps from this Indian when he was shot. * * * What you claim regarding yourself are undeniable facts."

Vernou (now Colonel C. A. Vernou, U. S. A.) says: * * * As soon as some of the horses which had stampeded the night before were caught and sent in from the front, we heard from the men about the man of Troop "G" being killed, and they told us of Lieutenant Carter's gallant behavior, and said if it had not been for his action *things would have gone pretty badly.* * * *"

There also follows a letter from one of the oldest and best First Sergeants in the Fourth Cavalry, later Ordnance Sergeant Joseph Sudsburger, U. S. A., retired, now dead:

To Whom It May Concern:

This is to certify that I was a Corporal of Troop "B," Fourth U. S. Cavalry, which Lieutenant R. G. Carter commanded (being specially detached from his own Troop "E" for that purpose) in the campaign against the Qua-ha-da Comanche Indians from October 2 to November 18, 1871. On the morning of October 10, 1871, the Indians stampeded our camp on the Freshwater Fork of the Brazos River, Texas.

While I did not participate in the action which followed later that morning, I know that the statement of Lieutenant Carter is absolutely true in every respect. I had knowledge of all the facts. It was common report among all the enlisted men in the regiment that had it not been for the great skill, cool judgment, and most conspicuous bravery of Lieutenant Carter in the action of that morning, every man of both his own and Captain E. M. Heyl's detachment would have lost their lives. Private Gregg was killed within a few feet of him, and Privates Melville and Downey of Troop "G" were wounded by his side.

I have full knowledge of all the facts connected with the serious injury which Lieutenant Carter received that morning by the falling of his horse when making a charge upon a body of Indian sharpshooters posted on a rocky bluff; of his riding five days with his leg in splints when in pursuit of this band of Indians; and of his treatment for such injury by A. A. Surgeon Rufus Choate, when the command was moving out. I have seen him often since 1887, and known of his suffering ever since.

I was with the command when it made its great raid into Mexico, May 17-19, 1873, and was present when a Lipan Indian, who was decoyed into the burning Kickapoo Village, by a Seminole Indian scout and not disarmed, tried to shoot Captain Mauck, who commanded my troop.

I saw Lieutenant Carter and a Corporal of Troop "M" shoot the Indian down, the former firing first, his shot turning him around and backward so as to throw up his rifle at the moment of discharge into the air, when he fell dead. Lieutenant Carter, by his prompt action, saved the life of Captain Mauck, and the act was witnessed by many officers and men in the command who were standing around the captured prisoners in groups.

Lieutenant Carter was always regarded in the regiment as one of its hardest worked, most efficient, and bravest officers, not only by the commissioned, but by the non-commissioned officers and enlisted men. His constant and valuable services, tireless energy, and conspicuously gallant conduct during those years of continuous Indian warfare, and his uniformly firm but kind treatment of the men in his troop, afforded an example and incentive which stimulated them to their best efforts and made the Fourth Cavalry, under the leadership of General Ranald S. Mackenzie, second to none in the entire Army. It was the only cavalry regiment that ever received the thanks of a State for its services in driving the Indians from its frontier counties.

And when the Army Appropriation Bill of 1877 failed in Congress, and the officers of the Army were without their pay for a period of about six months, in a letter which General Sherman wrote to General Mackenzie, at Fort Hays, Kansas, which I saw, he stated that the entire Texas delegation agreed to vote for the bill, provided General Mackenzie with the Fourth Cavalry should be ordered back to the Department with headquarters at Fort Clark, Texas.

JOSEPH SUDSBURGER,

Ordnance Sergeant, U. S, Army, Retired.

Late First Sergeant, Troop "B" Fourth U. S. Cavalry.

Sworn to and subscribed before me, a Notary Public for the District of Columbia, at Washington, D. C, this 29th day of April, A. D. 1904.

THOMAS J. SULLIVAN,

(seal.) *Notary Public, D, C.*

In 1896, Col. E. B, Beaumont was Acting Inspector General of the Department of Texas. At that time he made, at the request of the writer, a search for Mackenzie's report, and wrote the following letter:

SAN ANTONIO, TEXAS, *March 22, 1890.*

MY DEAR CARTER:

The Adjutant General is having copy made of Mackenzie's report, but, as I surmised, he made no mention of you or Boehm in his report, and on the contrary Heyl is reported as having driven the Indians several miles without bringing them to a fight. Possibly if he had been up when you and Boehm were in such a tight place he would have been able to participate in a fight. I am in exactly the same position as you and Boehm, for although I made the *entire* captures at the Palo Duro fight, having command of A and E Companies in the advance, and Boehm was with me, neither of us were mentioned in the report; in fact, it does not appear that we were there at all. * * * * I consider that to my part we owed all our successful captures. But I was never mentioned. * * * * in fact we were completely ignored. These reports have given me a view of Mackenzie's character that I never saw before. * * * * *De Mortuis Nil Nisi Bonum*" is the old adage, but as we all toiled and fought to advance him, it would have been a graceful act, to say the least, if he had said a pleasant word of praise for duty fairly performed. The lesson comes late in life and after we have borne the heat and toil of the day. No matter how hard we strove to do our duty and what hardships we had to undergo. You remember the fatigue of our Mexican trip. It was never known beyond our own orbit and I can now understand how little interest was expressed in us when we occasionally visited Washington.

War Department greeting:

"Ah, how are you, Jones?

"Where is your station? How long are you going to stay in the city? Good morning."

The fact is, I do not believe you can strengthen yourself by searching for commendations from Mackenzie, for he never wrote any, I think. The proper way, and only one now left, is to get the testimony of the officers who were with you, setting forth the facts of the case, and then get General Augur to recommend you. * * * * I would Wee the truth to be known about that fight. * * * * if the gentleman who "*skinned out*" for the ravine and left you in the lurch attempts any "Shenanigin" you must go before the Military Committee and tell the truth about the fight. I have always considered that you and Boehm, and I believe "Old Tone Henry," were the heroes of the fight and that you had a mighty dose call. * * *

Keep the greenest spot in your heart for me.

  Most truly your friend,

       (Signed) E. B. BEAUMONT.

R. G. Carter,
 U. S. Army.

A true copy.

Letter of Brigadier-General Wirt Davis, U. S. A. (then Captain Fourth Cavalry), now dead, follows. His reputation throughout the entire Army was that of being one of the bravest and most efficient officers in the cavalry service.

      BALTIMORE, MD., *December* 6, 1904.

To Whom It May Concern:

This is to set forth that Troop "F," Fourth U. S. Cavalry, of which I was then the captain, was one of the six troops of that regiment, Colonel R. S. Mackenzie, Brevet Brigadier General, U. S. A., commanding, that took part in the expedition in October and November, 1871, against the hostile Qua-ha-da band (Quoina's) of Comanche Indians, and that I was present during the whole campaign.

About sunset on the 9th of October, 1871, the command encamped on the Freshwater Fork of the Brazos River, Texas. About 1 o'dock a. m. on the 10th of October, 1871, as the moon was setting, a considerable number of mounted Comanches, yelling and firing pistols, charged past our camp and succeeded in stampeding some horses and mules. At daylight several officers with detachments of men were sent out by Colonel Mackenzie to search for and recover the stampeded animals. . . . . A large party of Comanches suddenly attacked Captain Heyl's troop while hunting for the loose horses, killed one of his men, but were assailed and driven off by Lieutenants Carter and Boehm, who, with their detachments, promptly and gallantly rushed to Heyl's relief . Colonel Mackenzie, when the firing was heard, ordered me to mount my troop (the horses were already saddled), and with him I proceeded at a gallop toward the scene of conflict. When we arrived there, however, the Indians had scattered and had fled up the Freshwater Fork of the Brazos toward the Staked Plains. Lieutenant Carter, while pursuing the Indians who had attacked Captain Heyl's troop, was badly injured by his horse falling and jamming his leg against a rode. The injury was a serious one, and it was so pronounced to be by Acting Assistant Surgeon Rufus Choate, U. S. A., who attended him. Although I was not an eye-witness of the mishap that befell Lieutenant Carter in the affair with hostile Comanches on October 10, 1871, yet I know that he was injured as described herein. Lieutenant Boehm, who was first lieutenant of my Troop "F," but who on that expedition was chief of scouts for Colonel Mackenzie, related all the facts and circumstances in the case to me in camp on the following day and subsequently often referred to the matter in conversation with me. It may not be irrelevant for me to state that Lieutenant Carter was known in the Fourth Cavalry as a *very energetic and gallant officer*, and his involuntary and reluctant retirement from the service on account of disability in the line of duty was regarded by *many officers as a decided loss to the regiment.*

WIRT DAVIS,
Brigadier General, U. S. Army,
Retired, In 1871—Captain, Troop "F," Fourth U. S. Cavalry.

In a personal letter to Captain Carter, General Wirt Davis adds the following:

DEAR CARTER:

Enclosed with this is a statement concerning the affair on the Freshwater Fork of the Brazos River, Texas, and although *it is not as strong as I would like to make it*, still I hope it may help you in securing favorable action on your petition. I have read the brief very carefully, and it is a lucid and forcible statement of reasons why an enabling act of Congress should be passed authorizing the President to appoint you a Colonel, U. S. Army, mounted, to date from January 30, 1903. You certainly deserve consideration for your service in the War of the Rebellion and in the arduous Indian campaigns after that memorable war. I sincerely hope that you may be successful in obtaining special legislation for your relief.

The foregoing letters are from every officer of the Fourth U. S. Cavalry now living who was with Captain Carter in the Indian campaign of 1871.

Life is full of "ifs." They are the turning points in our career. "If" is a little word, but is a big factor. "If" the writer had realized what that report of Mackenzie's was to have been and what it would mean to him, his answer to the question put to him in Cañon Blanco would have been of a far different nature. In his generosity to avoid smirching or blasting a brother officer's career, an injustice was done to him and his truly brave, generous rescuer, which now, after a lapse of 48 years, is just being set right. It is this little word "if" that makes life, after all, a gamble.

"If "it should be said that this is a case of the "donkey kicking the fallen lion," the answer might be "see yourself in the mirror," or, read Charles Reade's *"Put Yourself in His Place."*

Some men are like counterfeit or spurious coins. But, by self-advertising or the undue influence of sycophantic friends, they sometimes manage to retain their purchasing power, and remain at their face value, even though oftentimes they have been known to be failures or to achieve success in any way. This has been accomplished by the P. T. Barnum process of everlasting talk, newspaper twaddle, and red and yellow posters. There is, it seems necessary to repeat, a great deal of hypocrisy, cant, Barnum humbuggery and hysteria in this country, and in no place is it more in evidence than in the Capital. The writer has gained this knowledge by a close observation of more than 30 years directly in contact with the machinery by which this Government is supposed to function. No close observing man, with ample time on his hands, could remain in Washington during both the Spanish-American and this World War just closing without gaining this knowledge—almost at first hand—or being fully impressed with the startling truth of the psychological developments of both of these war periods, with their excitement, "endless chain" methods, emotional frenzy, and hero worship.

Medal of Honor: "Most Distinguished Gallantry"—Brevet: "Specially Gallant Conduct"

The writer, many years after this affair, was accorded partial justice by being awarded the Congressional medal of honor, the officers of the Fourth Cavalry practically uniting in an endorsement on the following application made by Major P. M. Boehm, then Captain U. S. A., retired*

WASHINGTON, D. C., December 13, 1893.

TO THE ASSISTANT SECRETARY OF WAR,
Washington, D. C.

SIR:

I have the honor to recommend and to request that First Lieutenant and Brevet Captain R. G. Carter, U. S. A., retired, may be awarded a medal of honor for conspicuous gallantry and bravery in action with Qua-ha-da Comanche Indians on the Freshwater Fork of the Brazos River, Texas, on the morning of October 10, 1871.

I have read Lieutenant Carter's statement and it is correct in every respect. I was present at the time the Indians made their last charge upon him and his little command, and can vouch for the *conspicuously brave conduct, skill, and good judgment* shown by Lieutenant Carter. * * *

If any distinguished honor is to be bestowed upon any officer engaged at the time herein mentioned. Lieutenant R. G. Carter is clearly entitled to it, as his act was entirely voluntary, he being officer of the day at the time, and on a tour of the pickets when he first sighted the Indians which he and the other officers chased with their commands until they met the main body.

I have the honor to be, sir.

Very respectfully, your obedient servant,

(*Signed*) P. M. BOEHM,

Captain, U. S. A., Retired.

This medal of honor was awarded the writer for *"Mos Distinguished Gallantry* in action against Indians on Brazos (Freshwater Fork) River, Texas, October 10, 1871, in holding the left of the line with a few men during the charge of a large body of Indians, after the right of the line had retreated, and by delivering a rapid fire, succeeded in checking the Indians until other troops came to the rescue, while serving as Second Lieutenant, Fourth Cavalry."

Under the act of Congress of February 27, 1890, granting Indian brevets for gallantry, the writer was given the brevet of First Lieutenant, U. S. Army, for *"Specially Gallant Conduct* in action against Indians on the Brazos (Freshwater Fork) River, Texas, October 10, 1871," and later the brevet of Captain, U. S. Army, for "Gallant Services in action against Kickapoo, Lipan, and Mescalero Apache Indians at Remolino, Mexico, May 18, 1873."

Quan-ah Surrenders—Adobe Walls—Palo Duro

The expedition into the Texas panhandle in 1874 of four columns, operating from the north, south, east, and west, and resulting in the actions near Red River on September 27-28, and at Las Lagunas Quatro and at the Palo Duro on November 5, 1874, and Quan-ah's disastrous defeat by the destruction of his villages and the wholesale killing of nearly two thousand ponies, which had been captured from him, a whole day being devoted by Lawton to shooting them, one troop being detailed for that purpose—the pile of bones being still there, according to reports of the inhabitants of that region to the writer—forced Quan-ah to come in and surrender early in 1875. Just prior to these fights, however, Quan-ah made one last desperate effort to hold his Indians together, and through his influence and wily diplomacy succeeded in persuading all of the bands of the Comanche and Cheyenne tribes with about half of the Ki-o-was and other Indians to affiliate with him and make an attack upon an organized company of white buffalo hunters whom he claimed were depredating upon the well recognized Indian lands over which the immense herds of buffalo grazed, and upon which the Indians then relied for almost their very existence in lodge-skins, clothing, food, etc. He mustered about seven hundred warriors, and the campaign began June 24, 1874, with an attack led by Quan-ah in person with his confederated Indians, against the buffalo hunters, who were strongly intrenched in a rude fort known as the Adobe Walls, on the South Canadian in the Texas panhandle. In addition to the thick

105

walls, the hunters had a small field piece which they used with such good effect that after a siege lasting all day the Indians were obliged to withdraw with considerable loss. Most of the hostiles then surrendered, but Quan-ah, implacable to the last, kept the Qua-ha-das (Kwahadi band) out till the last, when these four converging columns finally administered the death blow to him and his Indians, "the *Vanishing Race.*"

Quan-ah as a "Good Indian"—His Reward—Another Romance—His Death—Last Rites

Quan-ah lived, after "coming in," at the Fort Sill Reservation. To placate him, and keep him on the "good road," so that he might follow the white man and be a useful member of society, he was given land, horses, mules, and cattle, and a substantial two-storied house to live in. This house had a large star on the roof, to distinguish it, presumably, from the other houses, and was about twelve or fifteen miles from the town of Lawton. He leased his land to cattlemen for grazing purposes, and, in this way accumulated a large fortune for an Indian. He rode in state (four-mule ambulance) with his squaws—of whom he had, it was reported, at one time seven—and twenty-two children. He came to Washington many times, and at Theodore Roosevelt's second inauguration, in 1905, the writer saw him ride up Pennsylvania Avenue in the inaugural column with other "good Indians," most of whom had dipped their hands in many a white settler's blood on the once far off borderland of the West.

On February 10, 1908, Hon. John H. Stephens, Member of Congress from Texas, offered a bill appropriating one thousand dollars for a memorial to Cynthia Ann Parker in Texas, offering the following as his reason: "In view of the *public service* rendered by this Indian (Quan-ah) to the white people on the Texas frontier, in *causing his tribe* to quit the war path and live on their reservation, and the further fact of the suffering of his mother for so many years as a white captive among the savages." This was done at the request of Quan-ah, then in Washington, in behalf of his mother, who had died about 1864, and his infant sister, Prairie Flower, both of whom had been buried in the Fosterville cemetery, near Poyner Station in Henderson County, Texas. This bill was passed on the Indian Appropriation Bill on the same day. Quanah then had ample means to erect this memorial.

The Texas authorities having refused Quan-ah permission to remove the bodies of his mother and sister to his new home, he, accompanied by C. W. Birdsong, Indian agent, and son-in-law of Quan-ah, on November 29, 1910, smuggled the bodies from their graves, and brought them to Cache, about twelve or fifteen miles west of Lawton, near Fort Sill, Oklahoma.

Quanah died February 22, 1911, of an attack of asthma and rheumatism, leaving three wives and fifteen children. He was reputed to be the wealthiest Indian in the United States, through the generosity of the Government. He was buried at Post Oak Mission Cemetery, near Lawton, on February 24, 1911. The reburial of his mother had been postponed for the following Sunday, and it had been planned that Quan-ah should perform the ceremony, but his sudden death interrupted these plans. At sunrise on the morning of his death, the real Indian burial ceremony began. Three times dining the night, "Too-nicey," the favorite of Quanah's remaining three squaws, arose and loudly called to the Great Spirit for her chief. At five o'clock, crying loudly, "This is the time I always build a fire for him," she waked all the family. At six o'clock, Marcus Poco, Chief Medicine Man of the tribe and preacher, conducted the "sunrise funeral," crying to the Great Spirit and to the white man's God to accept the spirit of the dead chief. The Indians chanted weird dirges. More than one thousand attended, including hundreds of Indians.

The body of Quan-ah was dressed in his buckskin suit of former days. At noon the funeral party wended its way among the hills of the Parker ranch to the little Indian cemetery, and the funeral service began. A. J. Breaker (or Becker), Mennonite missionary, conducted it after the manner of the whites. Following this, the Indians sang the "swan Song," the Medicine Man again cried to the Great Spirit, and the body was lowered to the side of his white mother. In the coffin were placed a buckskin bag containing Quan-ah's favorite feathers, his war bonnet, trinkets, and jewelry. Among the latter was a diamond brooch, valued at $450, the present of cattlemen who had grazed their stock on the Comanche ranges fifteen years before, and became rich.

Nacona, a town named after Quan-ah's father, is on the M. K. & T. R. R., in Montague County, a few miles south of Old Spanish Fort on the Red River.

Quanah, a town in the Texas panhandle, some miles east of Cañon Blanco, the county seat of Hardeman County, not far from the town of Vernon on Pease River, is named for him, the latter town being near where Peta Nacona, his father, was killed, and where his mother was recaptured by Captain Ross' rangers. Has anybody ever heard or known of other county seats in the Texas panhandle being named for any officers of the Fourth United States Cavalry, who risked their lives and sacrificed their health and future happiness here on earth in more than one effort to drive out that savage Qua-ha-da Comanche band and open up that wild and desolate region to settlement, civilization, wealth, and all the material prosperity it now enjoys, and which that wily Indian was seeking to prevent by bloody incursions, burning, plundering, and savage orgies?

A Retrospect

It has been said by wise men, great writers, sages, and ancient philosophers that one should never regard the past, or look or turn backward, but always live in the present, and look forward to one's future life, the past being forever dead and buried. That is excellent advice and philosophy for youth. Few young people do look backward, for their interest centers in their present work and ambitions, and their future lies before them full of gilded hopes and promises. But this chunk of wisdom does not always hold true with the aged for, while they are compelled to adjust themselves to the present, there are few, if any, rosy promises held out to them for a future—unless, with full faith, it is the one after life—especially if some event in that past life has been largely responsible for much of the sorrow, bitter disappointments, and blasted hopes in their selected career and life profession, or, for past and present danger, physical pain and daily suffering.

These same historical writers and wise men frequently quote that old Latin adage, *"de mortuis nil nisi bonum"* (say nothing but good of the dead). That is also a good philosophy if not carried too far, and provided it does not work too much injustice to the living. We have been living for years in a crazy age of grotesque humbuggery, of fraud, of sham, and "faking." It has smacked strongly of the P. T. Barnum age, that great showman, who once wrote a book on how to "fool" and "humbug" the great American people. It has been the age of false pretension, of "hypnotism," of "fads," and "mind reading," "absent treatment," "theosophy," "spiritualism," and the "occult," etc. An age of "cure alls." Some years since the writer called attention in a book which he had published, "Four Brothers in Blue," to the battle of Chancellorsville, in which he was engaged, where a drunken commanding general imperilled the lives of his entire Army by his conduct. He held eighty thousand men's lives in the hollow of his hand, and for more than two days that magnificent old Army of the Potomac was without a commander or a leader. The latter was lying *spineless, inactive,* and *inert* in his tent, while the gallant men in that Army, ready to do and dare, were humiliated by being held in an almost paralyzed condition for lack of that leadership. If anybody dared to speak or come out in print and give, from their own knowledge, the true cause for such a woeful condition, he was immediately assailed, and this old Latin saying was sprung on him, "Say nothing but good of the dead," in an effort to "whitewash" and stifle criticism of the one man who was really responsible for such an act, and the never-to-beforgotten and disgraceful disaster which followed as a result, and for which we all had to suffer indescribable hardships as well as unnecessary humiliation through *his* failure to achieve success either through criminal carelessness and neglect, or *his* weakness and moral and mental unfitness to assume such responsibilities.

While there are probably none who would not gladly subscribe to the ethics of the wise adage just quoted, because it is a truth which few would or could seek to disregard, yet there is something beyond and greater than this in its practical application, and that is a living force.

It is *justice*, without which life is a travesty, a farce, and a hollow sham. *Justice to the living;* for there were, and are today, many real victims of the acts of the dead, and it is worse than folly to feign blindness or knowledge of the truth. It is a crime!

There are men living today who saw the author of that disgrace lying impotent and nerveless in his tent by the side of the little white house (Bullock's) near the intersection of the Ely's Ford and the United States Ford roads, and have lived to see an equestrian statue in bronze erected in commemoration of ids deeds near the State House in Boston. But no soldier who was in the battle line at Chancellorsville and near enough to this self-exalted commanding general of the old Army of the Potomac to see his condition, will ever forget what took place there during those fateful hours (May 2-6, 1863) with nobody in command, or, now the "grotesque humbuggery" of perpetuating this man's memory, or such a deed, in the face of what we knew then, and what we had to endure on account of the same. Even his adjutant general, who was for years in one of the Departments in Washington, admitted the urgent need of stimulating him when it was seen that he had "lost his grip" on the situation, but, in doing so, realized that they had, unfortunately, exceeded the limit and rendered him *hors de combat*. Upon being asked by General Doubleday sometime after the battle what was the matter with him during that crisis. Hooker's reply was, "The shock I received by shell concussion at the Chancellor House did not injure me, I was not drunk, but I was not, on that day, 'fighting Joe Hooker.' " And everybody was free to draw their own conclusions, except those alone who knew the facts, having seen all with their own eyes, and there were many who did see and know.

The case, given in illustration, can be applied with full force, and in all its meaning, to the writer's case in connection with the tragedy of Cañon Blanco. He has been urged many times to tell the true story, even if necessary to the committees of Congress, before the medal of honor was awarded him, and especially in view of Mackenzie's most amazing report, which was not known of for a number of years. Nobody can fully analyze, not even a soldier, another man's thoughts, his feelings, or sensations at a moment of extreme danger, a sudden crisis, or his mental, physical, and moral attitude. Much less is he able to control them. But he can analyze that man's acts who, being impelled by some sudden impulse or force has lost control of himself, so far as it may affect another's life, his hopes, ambitions, and future prospects. Is one always to live a life of suffering and injustice when it has been brought about by the wrong-doing and deliberate acts of the dead, who, when living, never by word or deed gave expression of regret for such act, except to an intimate friend in a moment of confidence and, perhaps, of remorse? In this case the commanding officer was not drunk. He simply lost his head—went off in a blue "funk"—became panic stricken—fled the field and left the writer not only to suffer the consequences of such an act at the moment, but to be punished and be the victim for the balance of his life, with no remedy except through the generosity of his brother officers in securing him the medal of honor and a brevet as a matter of justice, after all the facts had been known, verified, and sworn to by them.

Then why this cry of "*de mortuis nil nisi bonum?*" What about the living, especially when they have had to suffer for the mental, physical, and moral attitude of the dead—their lapses and lack of decisive action? Is something not due to them if their lives have been so closely interwoven with the acts of the dead as to make it practically impossible to separate or dissociate their present and past, if not their future, lives from those acts? Forty-eight years have passed, but the human mind is utterly incapable of assuming the task of forgetting under all the circumstances this tragedy of Cañon Blanco.

The world moves in cycles or periods, psychological periods or eras of "farces," *"shams," "isms," "cults," "endless chains," etc. Every such recurring cycle or period has its insincere, two-faced hypocrites—some humbug, like a Barnum—to make the world pay for its humbuggery; some idealist or dreamer who pleads for an Eutopia or the millenium; some prophet who predicts the approaching end of the world; or a Bolshevist or Anarchist who preaches anarchy, destruction, and chaos. Wars have been a most prolific source of such a worldwide craze, of frenzied hysteria, of license, camouflaging under the mask of liberty, of hero worship, and of personal adulation to a sickening extent, *ad nauseam*.

In every age, and in the cycles and periods of that age there have been charlatans, frauds, shams, fakes, and humbugs, and the people have been "fooled," "flim-flammed," "hoodooed," or "buncoed" ever since the world begun, and still there are among them some wise sages and philosophers who still cry out *"de mortuis nil nisi bonum,"* and the world moves on—stumbling, blundering, bungling along toward its ultimate mission, the mystery of which we mortals, poor little ants, know not of. We had these conditions during the Civil War, during the Indian wars, the Spanish-American war. It was present in the campaign after Quan-ah's band, and in the action at Cañon Blanco. The word "camouflage" had not then come into use as a military term. All of these strange conditions were "camouflaged" under another name which even Barnum himself would never have recognized as "humbug." When Mackenzie made that strange and meager report of the expedition of 1871, he had, perhaps unconsciously, come under the influence of this camouflage. We might as well call it by its right name. He had either been completely humbugged, or had come under a spell of "hypnotism," or else his star had even then begun to set in the overshadowing darkness of a clouded night, and later, when the mental and physical strain had been too great, the "silver chord was loosed," the "golden bowl was broken."

To the Memory of Gen. R. S. Mackenzie.

Mackenzie, thy warfare is o'er—
    Thy bold, loyal heart is at rest.
Thy noble soul suffers earth's sorrows no more,
For thy bark sailing seaward has reached the lone shore
    Of that far-away land of the blest.

Brave hero, we mourn not for thee.
    Thou hast gone from life's troubles and care;
Thy stern, soldier spirit forever is free;
It has joined the Grand Army encamped by the Sea
    In the bivouac realms over there!

And yet since by love thou wert slain,
    In pity we bow o'er thy bier,
And we sigh when we think of thy story of pain,
Of that proud, loyal love that thou lavished in vain.
    And in secret we shed the sad tear.

But we feel that affection like thine
    Is not lost 'neath the gloom of the sod.
That beyond the dark valley where love is divine,
It will glow evermore and eternally shine
    In the balm-breathing Edens of God.

Mackenzie, true soldier, good-by;
>The wind wails thy long reveille.
And tonight on the plains where the weird coyotes cry.
Far away o'er thy trail 'neath the tents of the sky,
>I breathe this slight tribute to thee.

The incidents and events of that period are all indelibly stamped and photographed upon the brain. Can any occult science, or hypnotic influence, or the lapse of time remove these impressions? Is it possible for the writer to relegate to obscurity, oblivion, or to "innocuous desuetude" that which has dwelt there during all of his younger days, of his middle life, and now, during the rapid approach of old age? It can not be! Human nature is poor indeed that will seek to befog or shield the act of any man, who himself acknowledged that he was in a state of *"blue funk," when that act had so much to do with the life of another man who has so grievously suffered thereby. It seems to admit of no argument, no matter how much the victim may deplore that act or hesitate during almost a lifetime to set it forth in its true light, with all of its dreadful consequences.

While these conditions, past and present, and the strange psychological periods of sham, farces, humbugs, etc., already referred to, might not seem to the average reader to be in any way relevant to the subject-matter—a tragedy in Cañon Blanco, in the Texas panhandle—they all have a bearing upon this sham and shameful farce of an official report which credited two officers with an act which they not only did not perform, as has been shown by letters and affidavits of all the surviving officers of the Fourth Cavalry, but, by the only two eyewitnesses of that act, they reflected nothing but discredit to themselves, upon their regiment, and the entire Army, and had these officers not repudiated such a report, which must have been initiated under a disguise of sham, fraud, fake, and a frame-up, Heyl, upon a strict interpretation of that same report, had he not died, might have been awarded the medal of honor. The writer has seen almost as strange a case of official hypnotism and psychological flim-flam as this during his military career, as he actually knew of an amputation of the wrong limb during the Civil War, the victim of this sham operation never recovering his lost member or receiving any satisfaction for such loss.

It is hardly necessary to cite to the present generation the case of an extremely obese officer of our Regular Army, weighing over three hundred pounds—who had been unable to mount a horse for years—selected to actively (?) command our Army at Santiago during the Spanish-American war, or of all the distressing and painful complications arising therefrom, some of which have never been satisfactorily explained since. It was a clear case of P. T. Barnum's red and yellow poster advertising, of hypnotic camouflage, and official propaganda.

So much for *"de mortuis nil nisi bonum!"*

That affair in Cañon Blanco, the fight with the Comanche chief and his horde of wild savages, the misconduct of a brother officer, and the wreckage resulting therefrom was indeed the great tragedy of the writer's past life.

As a result of that terrible injury, and because surgical science at that period could not come to his relief, he was, after struggling along for several years, compelled to be retired at an age when most men are or should be most actively enjoying the prime and fullness of life. It has been a hard struggle ever since, because he was too sick to be able to take up the business activities which friends had opened up for him. Most of the expense of this sickness he bore out of his meager pay as first lieutenant, retired, while endeavoring, although in extremely wretched health, to support a wife and four children, eking out that same pay by doing school and college work, which, physically, he was unable to do without great risk to his life, although compelled to perform it by force of circumstances.

One hospital operation after another, while they saved his life, which for years was constantly in danger, never fully relieved him from the great handicap that hung like a great shadow over his life.

The leg was badly lacerated and bruised, thereby injuring the superficial veins, which shortly after began to enlarge and varicose. Subsequent hard service caused an extension of this enlargement above the knee and to the abdomen, and caused the valves of the large internal Saphenous vein to break down, forcing it to perform the duties of an artery. There was a constant tendency to rupture—it was similar to an aneurism of a large artery. While it was not a gunshot wound, its progressive effects were worse, far more reaching, from the fact that it not only caused him very great pain daily, and frequently endangered his life, but it seriously impaired his general health, and could not be checked nor relieved by the ordinary methods employed in skillful surgery, at that time, or for more than twenty-five years after, notwithstanding his frequent application for special treatment and such medical or surgical relief as the Surgeon-General's Office might afford, as is shown by his papers filed with the President.

The writer, by advice of Mackenzie, consulted the best medical and surgical authority at the Massachusetts General Hospital in Boston. He was examined by all the surgeons there (6), including Dr. Henry J. Bigelow, then at the head of his profession, and professor of surgery, etc., at Harvard University. On their united certificate, each having examined him separately, declaring that no radical operation would relieve him, and that any would be at too great a risk to his life, upon going before an Army Retiring Board, he was retired. One of these surgeons who signed that certificate, Doctor Porter, years later performed the first operation for the excision of the Saphenous vein by the Trendelenburg method, which the writer, after consultation with Major W. A. Borden, of the U. S. Medical Corps, had performed at the Washington Barracks General Hospital in March, 1901, after nearly thirty years of pain and constant danger almost unprecedented in the medical history of our Army. In addition to enlargement of the Saphenous vein, breaking down of the valves, etc., forcing the column of blood downward instead of its return to the heart, many other alarming symptoms had set in, such as neurasthenia, nervous indigestion, chronic insomnia, etc., the effects of which are still apparent. His case was demonstrated at the Washington Barracks Hospital before the class of officer medical students by Major W. C. Borden, Surgeon U. S. Army, January 22, 1903, who then declared that had these operations, by which Lieutenant Carter was relieved of his disability, been known in 1876, "*he need not have been retired.*" So successful had this operation been, however, that Colonel Borden gave the writer the following certificate:

(*Copy.*)
U. S. ARMY GENERAL HOSPITAL,
WASHINGTON BARRACKS,
WASHINGTON, D. C., *February* 10, 1903.

To Whom It May Concern:

I hereby certify that I operated upon Captain R. G. Carter, U. S. Army, retired, at the U. S. Army General Hospital, Washington Barracks, in March and June, 1901, for extensive varicose veins of the left leg, using the Trendelenburg and Schede operations, in the belief, as expressed at the time, that he would he greatly benefited if not permanently relieved, of his disability, but that it might be a year or more before the result would become fully apparent. I have recently examined Captain Carter and it is now my belief that he has been relieved of this disability.

(*Signed*) W. C. BORDEN,
Major and Surgeon, U, S. Army, Commanding Hospital.

A true copy; original filed with papers to the President.

The following statements of Dr. Rufus Choate are added to clearly indicate the serious nature of the injury received, its gradual progression, and efforts made to save the writer's life:

WASHINGTON, D. C, 310 Indiana Ave., *May* 3, 1890.

This certifies that I attended R. G. Carter, First Lieutenant, U. S. A., an officer of the Fourth U. S. Cavalry, while engaged in the pursuit of Comanche Indians in the campaign of 1871-72, under General Mackenzie, and especially on the morning of October 10, 1871, and for several days thereafter, for a severely injured leg.

I clearly remember the circumstance of the first examination. The command was in hot pursuit of Indians when Mr. Carter was injured. The leg was contused and greatly swollen, and the pain was so severe that I instructed the officer to remain on his horse while I examined the injured limb. I dismounted and found a condition that caused me more anxiety that I was disposed to exhibit. I expressed the opinion that probably a bone had been fractured, and I enclosed the leg then and there in a bandage, using the boot-leg as splints; believing that firmer splints would subsequently have to be applied.

I expressed the opinion that he would always suffer from the injury.

The case has frequently recurred to my mind as one of more than ordinary importance.

This officer was always a close applicant to duty. In the severe service required at that time by every one I may have given him attendance without carrying him on the sick list, but surely I must have made an entry of the case in my report to the Surgeon General.

Very respectfully,
RUFUS CHOATE, M. D.,
Late Acting Assistant Surgeon, U. S. A.

DR. RUFUS CHOATE.

THE FARRAGUT,
WASHINGTON, D. C., *February 18, 1903.*

Having again read the statement made by me in the case of Mr. R. G. Carter, Lieutenant, U. S. Army, at the date of May 3, 1890, 1 reafl&rm what is therein stated.

The gentleman has for many years been under my personal observation. The disability that began October lo, 1871 (in pursuit of Indians), had increased to an extent that was growing dangerous to life by beginning to varicose the veins within the abdomen, until the wonderfully skillful operation of Dr. W. C. Borden, Surgeon, U. S. Army, performed in March and June, 1901, has intervened, to which I believe Mr. Carter owes his life.

Very respectfully,

RUFUS CHOATE, M. D.,

Late Acting Assistant Surgeon, U. S. A.

Subscribed and sworn to before me this 25th day of February, 1903.

M. LeROY GOUGH,

(SEAL.) *Notary Public.*

If that operation was a success, and had restored him to a normal condition so that he could perform duty, why should he not have applied for restoration to the active list for duty which he not only knew he could perform, but in which he was sustained by one of the best medical officers of the Army? This, as a simple act of long-delayed justice, and as a reward for his past services? He did so, going with that certificate personally to the President, Theodore Roosevelt.

He would have been a captain June 30, 1883; a major July 5, 1898; a lieutenant-colonel February 17, 1901, and a colonel January 30, 1903, and by operation of law, could then have retired as a brigadier-general. In February, 1903, upon presenting a petition to the President setting forth all the facts in his case, citing all the precedents and asking for executive relief, and to be appointed to the grade he would have attained had he not been unfortunately retired, and alternatively expressing a desire for active duty in the field, the President assured him that *'any officer with such an exceptionally brilliant record, who had served during the Civil and Indian Wars, a graduate of West Point, who wore the medal of honor, was certainly entitled to *consideration*," and while he could not promise him the relief asked for, he would certainly go over his papers carefully, which he did, and discovering that he did not possess the executive power to grant the relief, without an enabling act of Congress, he so informed the writer, and urged him to take that action.

What "*consideration*" could the President have had in mind, were it not that for which he had just asked—a restoration to active duty? He practically said that any bill looking to that end would receive his hearty approval. And that is just exactly what he meant, for Theodore Roosevelt was no "four-flusher."

Then began the opposition, largely stimulated by greed, jealousy, and "sour grapes"; a rather hazy misunderstanding of the case; the underlying motives, etc. Through the do-nothing policy of a cold-blooded, discourteous, overrated, and obtuse militia chairman of the sub-committee on restorations, retirements, etc., of the Military Committee of the House of Representatives—the so-called guardian of the key to such bills—and an over-cautious Secretary of War, looking to the dollars and cents sacrificed (?) by a wealthy Nation in rewarding its Civil War and Indian fighters, this last act of injustice was finally perpetrated. When this effort was made for Congressional action to restore the writer to the active list as an extra number colonel for active duty he could then have well performed, the Secretary of War, Elihu Root, in reporting adversely, made the astounding declaration that while "this officer had a very enviable and most gallant record (with the M. H. and two brevets, etc.), a most generous Government had liberally provided for him by placing him on a retired list and rewarding him with the sum (computed down to the last cent by some pay expert designated for the purpose in the Pay Department) of ——— dollars, and he greatly feared that it would be establishing a bad precedent to advance him to the grade he would have attained could surgical aid have been secured sooner," etc. The Chief of Staff, General Chaffee, while strong in his praise of the writer's "gallant record," said practically the same thing, but to salve the writer's feelings, he was given a most munificent (?), but most strenuous, recruiting detail in the State of Alabama for two years, but with no increased rank. It was too strong a combination. Restoration of officers under the circumstances of a complete recovery for duty had been given in many instances, and numerous cases were cited, some with arms and legs off, in a brief, where such a restoration had been to the advantage of both Army and Navy. The writer would have had six of eight more years to his credit, and could then have retired at the age of sixty-four as a brigadier general. While it is believed to be true (and the contrary is challenged) that the writer then had the best fighting record among the graduates of West Point, either on the active or retired lists of the Army, and perhaps has it now, in view of this world war just terminating, these "medals," "badges," "brevet commissions," "grateful thanks," "letters of congratulation," "letters of commendation," "personal thanks," etc., "butter no parsnips," nor can they now compensate him for all the mental and physical anguish he has endured during this long period of years, through the many sacrifices he had made for his country, in view of his arriving at the age of seventy-four, and still on the list as a captain (about the only one at that age), and daily in contact with men of high rank—some of them made almost over-night—who, through no fault of their's, of course, have—some of them—never seen an Indian except a wooden image in front of a tobacco store, and who, even in this great world war, have never even been under rifle or shell fire, the battle statistics of that war showing that not one general officer in the A. E. F. was ever killed, wounded, shell-shocked, or scratched; while one hundred and twenty-three (123) general officers were killed or died of wounds in our Civil War. This is sad to contemplate, even as a retrospect, aside from hunger, thirst, hardships, privations, including the tragedy in that campaign.

This record of the writer's was earned in just two years and seven months of the most active field service which ever fell to the lot any cavalry officer—even in those days of strenuous duty—to perform. There are many officers on the active list of the army to-day, all of whom have come in since the Civil War, and most of them since the Indian Wars—who, after from 30 to 40 years, have no distinguished service record to their credit; merely the performance of perfimctory duty in garrison or in a swivel chair, and with almost phenomenal promotion. In this respect, therefore, length of service, with a mere performance of nominal duties, none of which disables or shortens one's life—will not compare with, nor will it bear the add test of, severity of field service within a prescribed limited period.

That any officer of the Army should, at seventy-four years of age, be on the retired list as a captain, with such a record, would, in any other country in the world, as we have seen in the cases of the German generals, Ludendorff, Hindenberg, and Von Mackensen, be almost an absolute impossibility, and in our's seems almost incomprehensible. At least it is pitiful in the extreme, especially when that captain is one of the last surviving few veterans of both the Civil and Indian Wars, the youngest of four brothers, who, starting in at Bull Run, terminated their services at Appomattox Court House, in their fight for the preservation of the American Union, and who aided in the defeat and surrender of this wily savage who never came in voluntarily to be such "a friend to the people of Texas and the Southwest" (as Mr. Stephens states) or to take up the "white man's burden," or camouflage under the hypocrisy of a suddenly acquired Christianity. Not until his band was driven from the fastnesses of the Palo Duro Cañon in 1874, Ws villages were destroyed, and his ponies were captured and shot, did he submit, relent, or repent. Then, seeing his ultimate fate, he "came in" and became a "good Indian." Generous Government, indeed! Could a generous Government afford to do less for a "gallant officer" of the Army who had almost sacrificed his life in an effort to promote the settlement of that wild, uninhabited, savage-infested territory, and to advance civilization in that now richest of rich countries, than it could later do for this murderous savage, so suddenly become converted to the white man's ways, but whose entire previous career had been devoted, not, as Mr. Stephens declared when asking for a $1,000 memorial to Quanah's mother, in "public service rendered by this Indian chief on the Texas frontier in causing his tribe to quit the warpath and live on their reservation," but in binning, pillaging, plundering, ravaging, and murdering every man, woman, or child who attempted to settle there. Did he (Mr. Stephens) ever dream that munificently rewarding an Indian chief on the ground of a sentimental gush, the brotherhood of man, or humanitarianism, who had murdered and scalped helpless women and children, was a worse precedent than in doing justice, although long delayed, to the officer who helped make him a "good Indian?" The two cases, the one considered by a Secretary of War, the other by the Member of Congress from Texas, are absolutely irreconcilable with the case of the writer, under any form of government, paternal or otherwise.

The writer did not ask for, or want to receive, "something for nothing," or to be a useless incubus upon the Army. He wanted to perform duty, only in a grade which he believed his years and experience entitled him to, even offering to go to the Philippines. If Congress, through such a sentiment for a so-called civilized (?) Indian, whose career had been marked by an orgy of blood and rapine, some of the foulest, darkest deeds ever recorded in the annals of Indian warfare, leaving always a trail of fire in his path, could bestow a $1,000 monument to honor the white mother who bore this implacable half-breed Comanche, and give him a Christian burial with imposing ceremonies (the writer has erected his own memorial in Arlington from the amount which Mr. Elihu Root declared a most generous Government had paid him for his wreckage), it could certainly have done a simple justice to the one officer who was so ready, for the sake of peace and civilization in that far-off Texas panhandle, to risk his life in what has, indeed, proved to be something more than a mere story, a chronicle of events, or a calm retrospect. It has become the supreme sacrifice, an almost life-long heritage of a real and truly great tragedy of Cañon Blanco.

CPSIA information can be obtained
at www.ICGtesting.com
Printed in the USA
LVOW04s1508300816
502491LV00039B/773/P